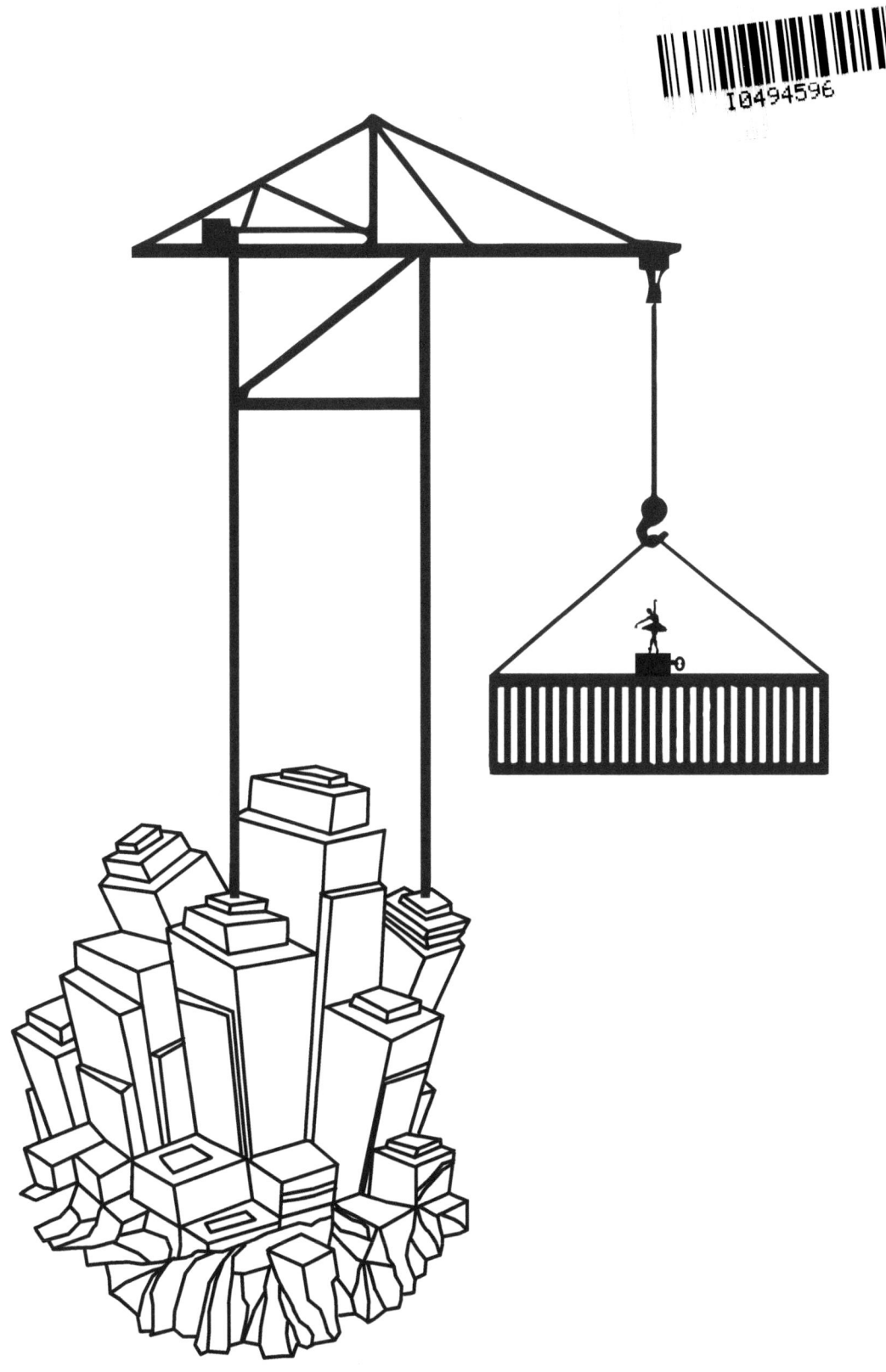

MORE&MORE (THE INVISIBLE OCEANS)
© 2016 Marina Zurkow

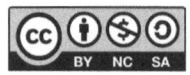

First published in 2016 by
punctum books
Earth
http://punctumbooks.com

punctum books is an independent, open-access publisher
dedicated to radically creative modes of intellectual inquiry
and writing across a whimsical para-humantities assemblage.
We solicit and pimp quixotic, sagely mad engagements
with textual thought-bodies. We provide shelters for
intellectual vagabonds.

More&More (The Invisible Oceans)
ISBN-13: 978-0692622001
ISBN-10: 0692622004

Cover: Marina Zurkow
Book design: Rebecca Lieberman
Code and craft: Sam Brenner, Xuedi Chen, Neil Cline,
Ariana Martinez, Justin Peake

Ocean image by Tiago Fioreze, licensed under CC BY 3.0

	Six-digit
0% or more calcalated on ct)	290122
in	291090
s in primary forms	390230
	290319
	290532
-dihydroxypropane) dicinal, preparations, bulk	300310-90
	291020
hyloxirane)	291020
n primary forms	392111-90
less than 90% pure	271129
less than 90% pure	271114
	292129
parations, bulk	300310-90
rations, bulk	300310-90
except preparations	293500
x, except preparations	293711-90
preparations, bulk	300310-90
ons, bulk	300310-90
preparations, bulk	300310-90
bulk, except preparations	293911-99
cept preparations	293911-99
	330499
baseball and softball	950699
hockey	950699
ubber, with a metal toe-	640110
except headwear, gloves, s	392620
	853641
made fibers, over 12	591190
dials, clock faces, etc.	701590
	853540
artificial filament,	

Prothesis, joint
Proton accelerators
Protoveratrines, bulk, except prepa
Protractors
Proustite ore
Provitamin a
Provitamin a, bulk
Provoloni, not grated, powdered, o
Proximity cards and tags
Prulose
Prune juice
Prune plums, fresh
Prunelles, dried
Prunelles, fresh
Pruners, tree, hand, not power–oper metal
Prunes, canned
Prunes, dried
Prunes, prepared or preserved, n.e.s.
Prunes, uncooked or cooked by stear boiling in water, frozen
Prunicodeine
Prussian blue
Prussic acid
Prydon
Pseudocumene, chemically defined c
Pseudoephedrine and its salts
Psilomelane ore
Psittaciformes (including parrots, para macaws and cockatoos)
Psophometers
Psychotherapeutic agents, dosage
Psychrometers, electric
Ptfe resin

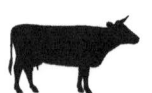

CHAPTER 1
Live animals

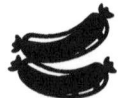

CHAPTER 2
Meat, edible meat offal

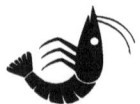

CHAPTER 3
Fish, crustaceans and mollusks

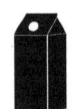

CHAPTER 4
Dairy produce; birds eggs; natural honey

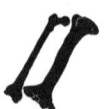

CHAPTER 5
Products of animal origin, not elsewhere specified or included

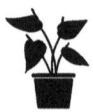

CHAPTER 6
Live trees and other plants; bulbs, roots; cut flowers; ornamental foliage

CHAPTER 7
Edible vegetables and certain roots and tubers

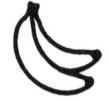

CHAPTER 8
Edible fruit and nuts; peel of citrus fruit or melons

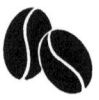

CHAPTER 9
Coffee, tea, maté and spices

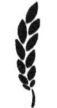

CHAPTER 10
Cereals

CHAPTER 11
Products of the milling industry; malt; starches; wheat gluten

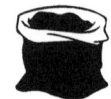

CHAPTER 12
Oil seeds; misc. grains, seeds and fruits; industrial or medicinal plants; straw and fodder

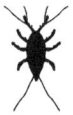

CHAPTER 13
Lac; gums, resins and other vegetable saps and extracts

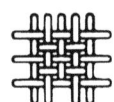

CHAPTER 14
Vegetable plaiting materials

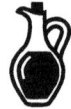

CHAPTER 15
Animal or vegetable fats and oils; animal or vegetable waxes

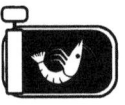

CHAPTER 16
Preparations of meat, fish, crustaceans or molluscs

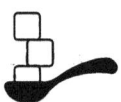

CHAPTER 17
Sugars and sugar confectionery

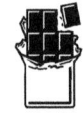

CHAPTER 18
Cocoa and cocoa preparations

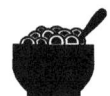

CHAPTER 19
Preparations of cereals, flour, starch or milk; bakers' wares

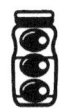

CHAPTER 20
Preparations of vegetables, fruit, nuts or other parts of plants

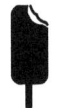

CHAPTER 21
Miscellaneous edible preparations

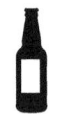

CHAPTER 22
Beverages, spirits and vinegar

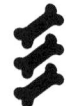

CHAPTER 23
Residues and waste from the food industries; animal feed

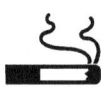

CHAPTER 24
Tobacco and manufactured tobacco substitutes

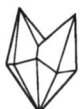

CHAPTER 25
Salt; sulfur; earths and stone; plastering materials, lime and cement

CHAPTER 26
Ores, slag and ash

CHAPTER 27
Mineral fuels, mineral oils and products of their distillation

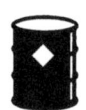

CHAPTER 28
Inorganic chemicals; compounds of metals

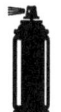

CHAPTER 29
Organic chemicals

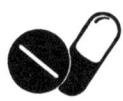

CHAPTER 30
Pharmaceutical products

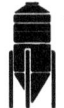

CHAPTER 31
Fertilizers

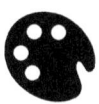

CHAPTER 32
Tanning or dyeing extracts; dyes, pigments, paints, varnishes, putty and mastics

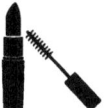

CHAPTER 33
Essential oils and resinoids; perfumery, cosmetic or toilet preparations

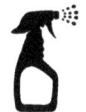

CHAPTER 34
Soap, organic surface-active agents; waxes, candles, modeling pastes

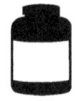

CHAPTER 35
Albuminoidal substances; modified starches; glues; enzymes

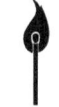

CHAPTER 36
Explosives; pyrotechnic products; matches

CHAPTER 37
Photographic or cinematographic goods

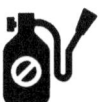

CHAPTER 38
Miscellaneous chemical products

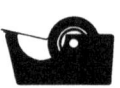

CHAPTER 39
Miscellaneous chemical products

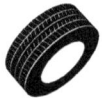

CHAPTER 40
Miscellaneous chemical products

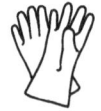

CHAPTER 41
Plastics and articles thereof

CHAPTER 42
Raw hides and skins (other than furskins) and leather

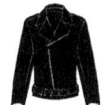

CHAPTER 43
Articles of leather; travel goods, handbags; articles of animal gut

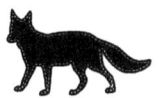

CHAPTER 44
Furskins and artificial fur; manufactures thereof

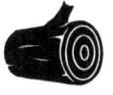

CHAPTER 45
Wood and articles of wood; wood charcoal

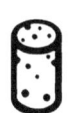

CHAPTER 46
Cork and articles of cork

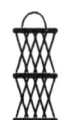

CHAPTER 47
Manufactures of straw or of other plaiting materials; basketware and wickerwork

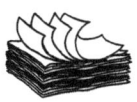

CHAPTER 48
Pulp of wood or of other fibrous material; waste and scrap of paper

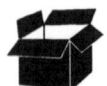

CHAPTER 49
Paper and paperboard; articles of paper

CHAPTER 50
Printed books, newspaper; manuscripts

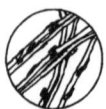

CHAPTER 51
Silk

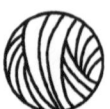

CHAPTER 52
Wool, fine or coarse animal hair; yarn and woven fabric

CHAPTER 53
Cotton

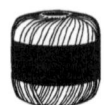

CHAPTER 54
Other vegetable textile fibers

CHAPTER 55
Man-made filaments

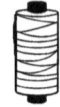

CHAPTER 56
Man-made staple fibers

CHAPTER 57
Wadding, felt and nonwovens; twine, cordage, ropes and cables and articles thereof

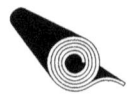

CHAPTER 58
Carpets and other textile floor coverings

CHAPTER 59
Special woven fabrics; lace, tapestries, trimmings

CHAPTER 60
Impregnated, coated, covered or laminated textile fabrics

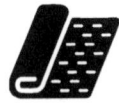

CHAPTER 61
Knitted or crocheted fabrics

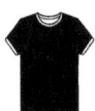

CHAPTER 62
Articles of apparel and clothing, knitted or crocheted

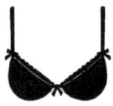

CHAPTER 63
Articles of apparel and clothing, not knitted or crocheted

CHAPTER 64
Other made up textile articles; worn clothing; rags

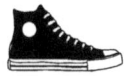

CHAPTER 65
Footwear, gaiters and the like; parts of such articles

CHAPTER 66
Headgear and parts thereof

CHAPTER 67
Umbrellas, sun umbrellas, walking sticks, seatsticks, whips, riding-crops

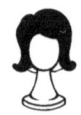

CHAPTER 68
Prepared feathers and down; artificial flowers; articles of human hair

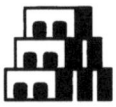

CHAPTER 69
Articles of stone, plaster, cement, asbestos, mica or similar materials

CHAPTER 70
Ceramic products

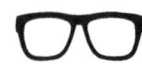

CHAPTER 71
Glass and glassware

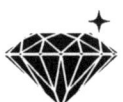

CHAPTER 72
Pearls, precious or semi-precious stones,precious metal; imitation jewelry; coin

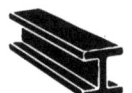

CHAPTER 73
Iron and steel

CHAPTER 74
Articles of iron or steel

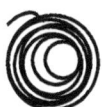

CHAPTER 75
Copper and articles thereof

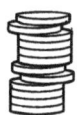

CHAPTER 76
Nickel and articles thereof

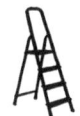

CHAPTER 77
Aluminum and articles thereof

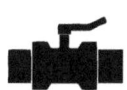

CHAPTER 79
Lead and articles thereof

CHAPTER 80
Zinc and articles thereof

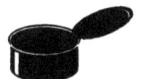

CHAPTER 81
Tin and articles thereof

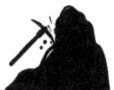

CHAPTER 82
Other base metals; cermets; articles thereof

CHAPTER 83
Tools, implements, cutlery, spoons and forks, of base metal

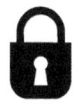

CHAPTER 84
Miscellaneous articles of base metal

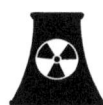

CHAPTER 85
Nuclear reactors, boilers, machinery and mechanical appliances

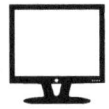

CHAPTER 86
Electrical machinery and equipment

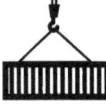

CHAPTER 87
Railway or tramway locomotives

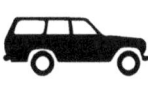

CHAPTER 88
Vehicles other than railway or tramway rolling stock

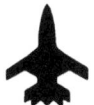

CHAPTER 89
Aircraft, spacecraft

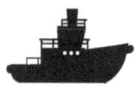

CHAPTER 90
Ships, boats and floating structures

CHAPTER 91
Optical, photographic, cinematographic, instruments

CHAPTER 92
Clocks and watches and parts thereof

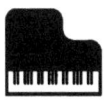

CHAPTER 93
Musical instruments

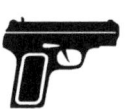

CHAPTER 94
Arms and ammunition

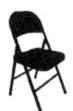

CHAPTER 95
Furniture; bedding, mattresses, cushions and similar stuffed furnishings

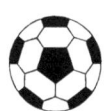

CHAPTER 96
Toys, games and sports requisites

CHAPTER 97/98
Miscellaneous manufactured articles; works of art, antiques

Humans know more about Mars than about the oceans.

The question at issue is...the OCEAN, that expanse of water
which antiquity describes as the immense, the infinite, bounded
only by the heavens, parent of all things...the ocean which,
although surrounding this earth, the home of the human race,
with the ebb and flow of its tides, can be neither seized nor
enclosed; nay, which rather possesses the earth than is by it
possessed.

– Grotius, Mare Liberum (The Freedom of the Seas), 1609

The jurist and philosopher Hugo Grotius wrote this gushing
passage as part of his tract, "Mare Liberum," to assert that
oceans are international territory, effectively using the ocean
as a poetic conceit, in order to utilize it as a surface for trade.
This was the first significant push for globalization and ocean
transport.

MORE&MORE, VALENTINE'S DAY, 2016, BITFORMS GALLERY, NY

MORE&MORE (the invisible oceans) is an art and research
project that explores the language and mechanics of global
trade, container shipping, and the exchange of goods,
questioning a mercantile structure that by necessity disallows
the presence of the ocean as a real space in order to flatten the
world into a Pangaea of capital.

Maritime shipping is a leviathan – opaque and illegible to
the non-expert, a system of codes and loopholes in which no
person has a picture of the entirety. The studio, initially driven
by an impulse to picture global, local and maritime spaces,
spent a year looking for legal and illegal data sources, getting
a rudimentary grasp on trade, visiting the Port of NY/NJ,
and digging away at the astounding scale and mechanics of
maritime shipping. We found patterns, literally, as we navigated
this "black box" of containerization.

The tunnel into this world lay in our discovery of the Harmonized
Commodity Description and Coding System (HS Code), the
internationally accepted standard of product classification,
which codifies the way nations conduct import/export. All
legal trade products (and illegal ones that find loopholes) are
shipped using this system. The studio translated this code to

use throughout our own expressive system, scraping data and
transforming it into icons and sculptures.

This claustrophobic fire-wall of HS Code generated the works
that make up this first installment of More&More: hypnotic,
generative animations of eight port nations' cultural and product
identities; a kiosk of top export items sculpted in fungus,
chocolate, soap; unique bathing suits visualizing import/export
data, a commerce web site, and the HS Code rendered as
wallpaper.

With this work, the ocean's absence is amplified – there
is little sense of the sea in this work, yet there are ships,
weather, waves. We uneasily connect to the "ever more and
more" feedback loop of commerce, and its indifference to
relational and natural systems. There are always chickens in
the supermarket and t-shirts on the rack. This "ocean in the
room" is the space outside the HS Code, outside the products,
the 24/7 maritime shipping apparatus, and outside the relentless
imperative to produce what's called "Productive Knowledge."
Our impulse was to magnify this hidden and labyrinthine
world – overwhelming, illegible, and absurd – as a starting
point for what will doubtlessly be a long course of work and
discovery.

There is a twin book to this catalogue: More&More (A Guide
to the Harmonized System), an experimental "brick" of a book
intervening in the Harmonized System code, with contributions
by scholars, theorists and poets.

– Marina Zurkow

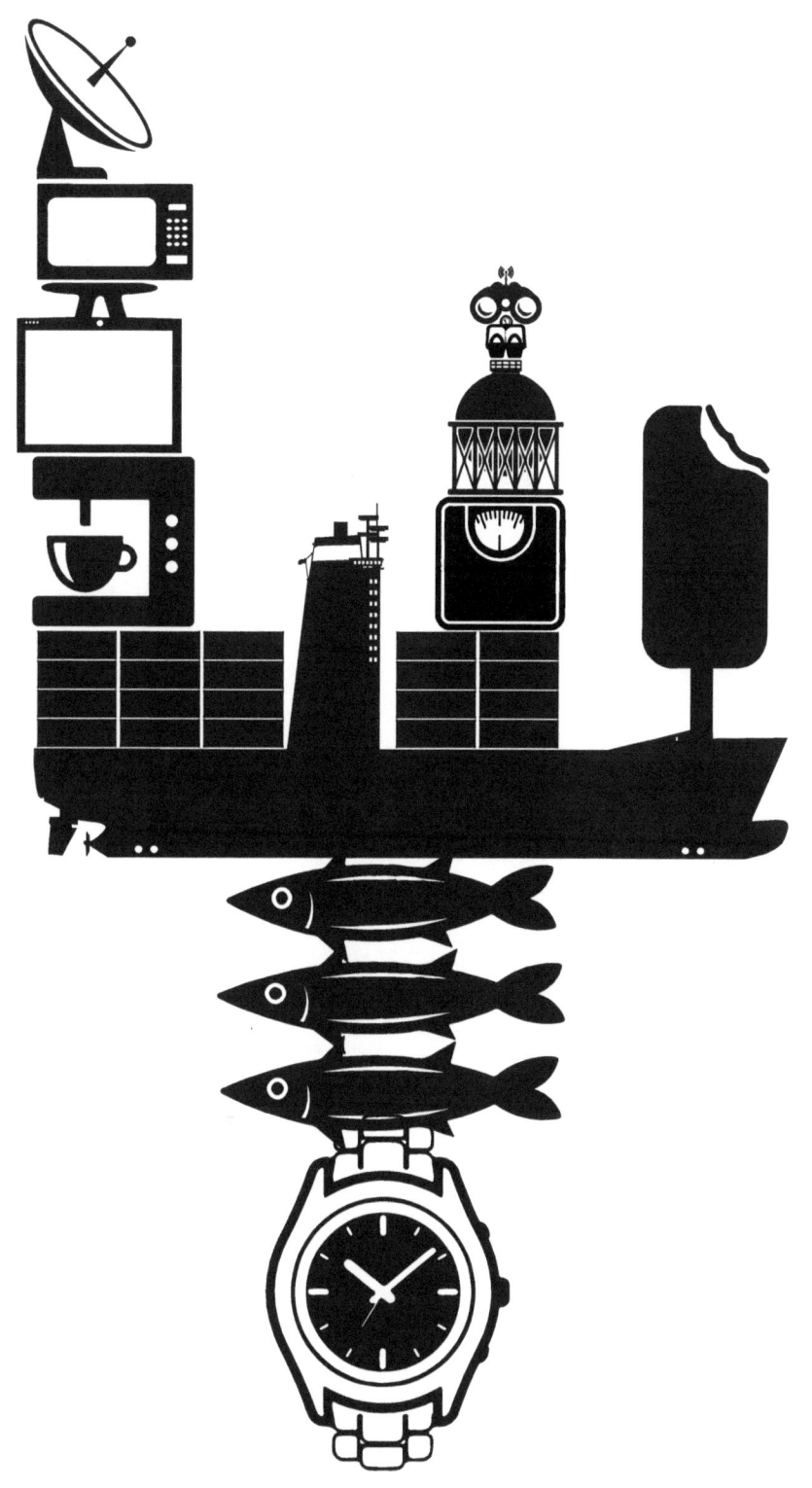

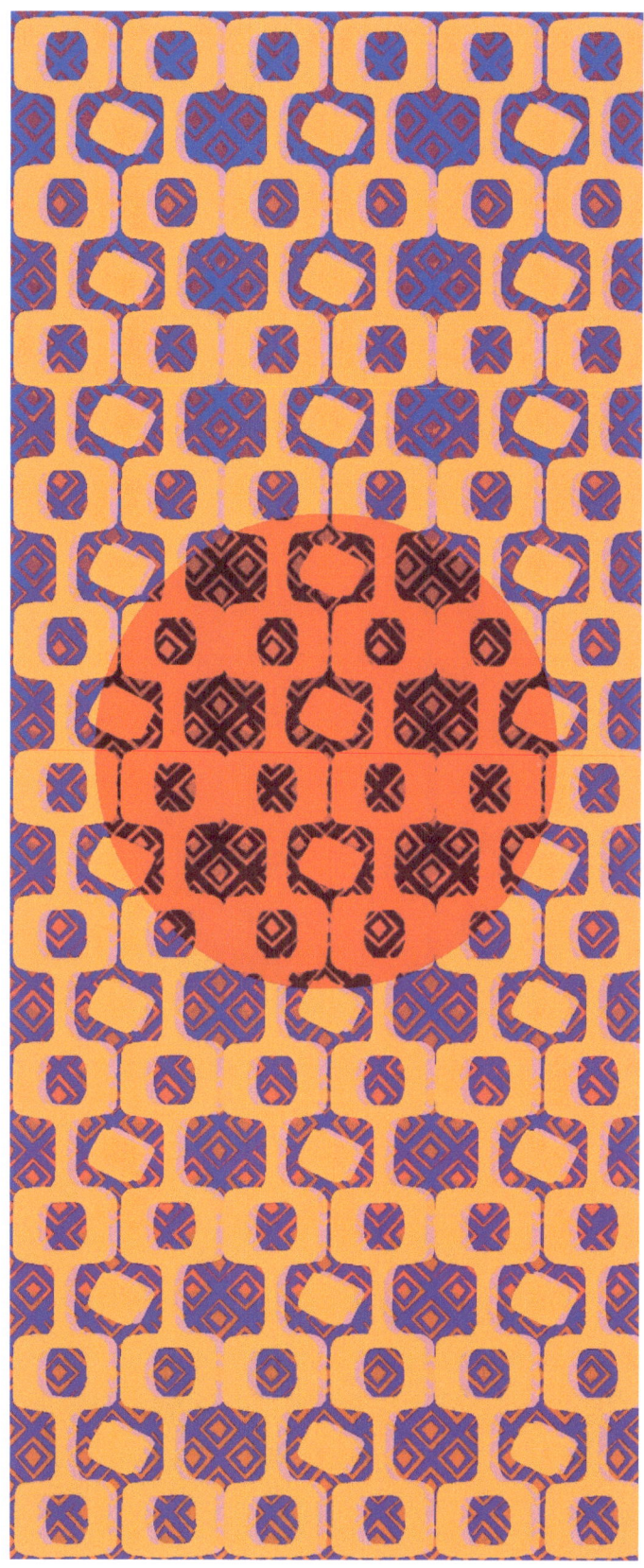

MORE&MORE (the invisible oceans):
Brazil
Software driven animation
Color, sound
Dimensions variable
Edition of 3
2016

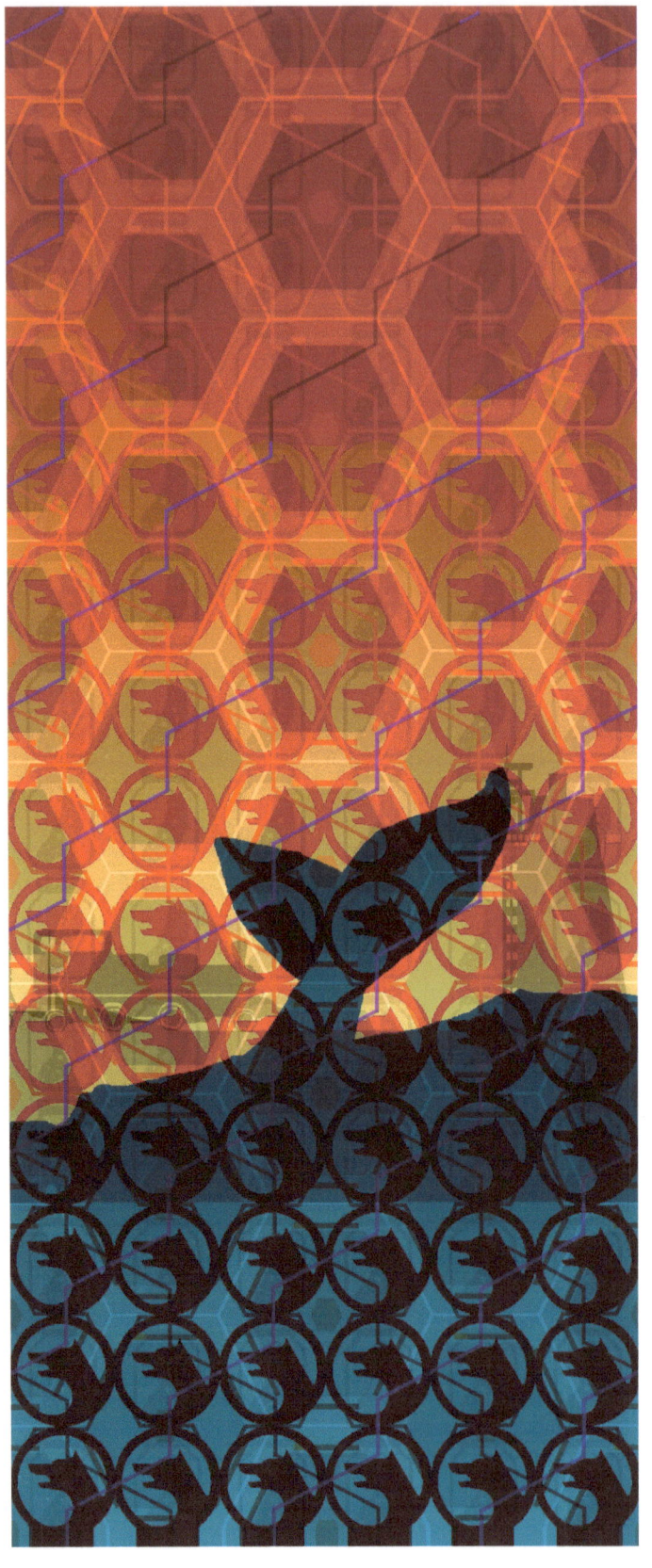

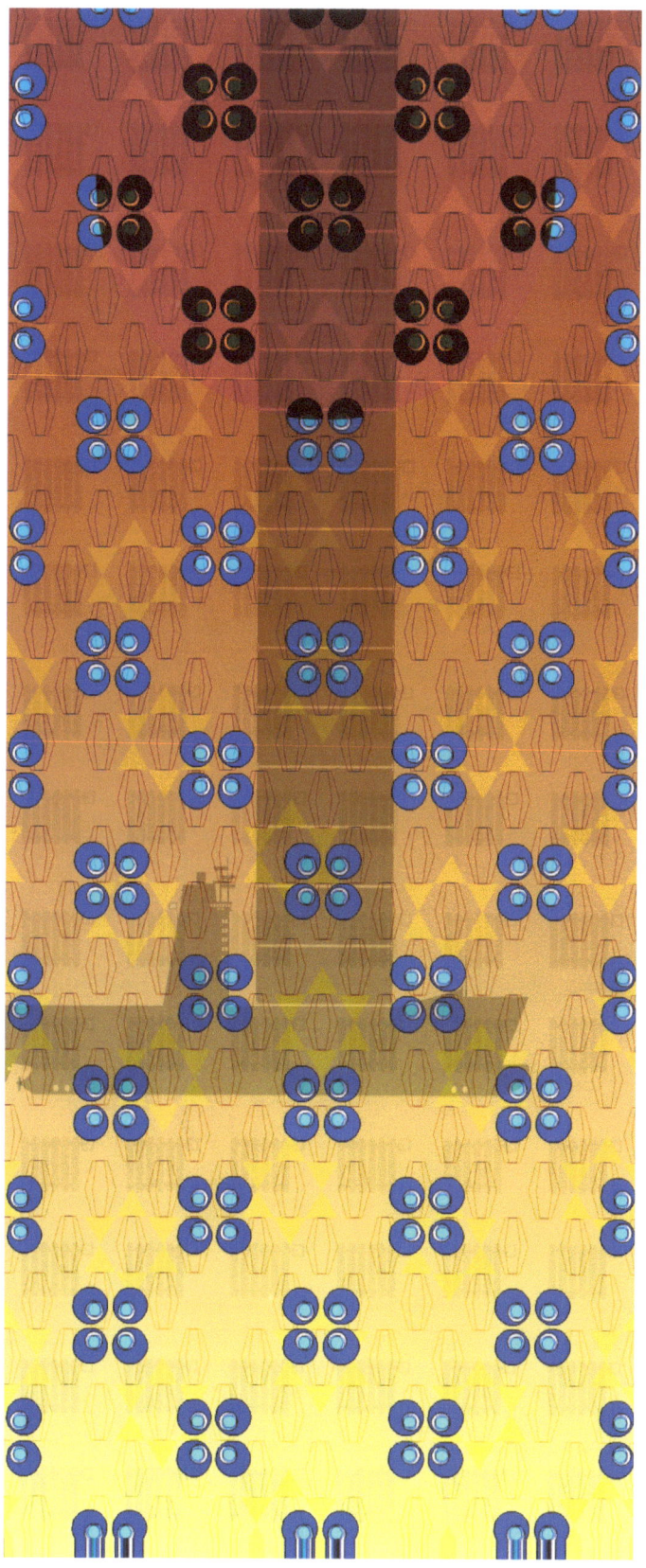

MORE&MORE (the invisible oceans):
Turkey
Software driven animation
Color, sound
Dimensions variable
Edition of 3
2016

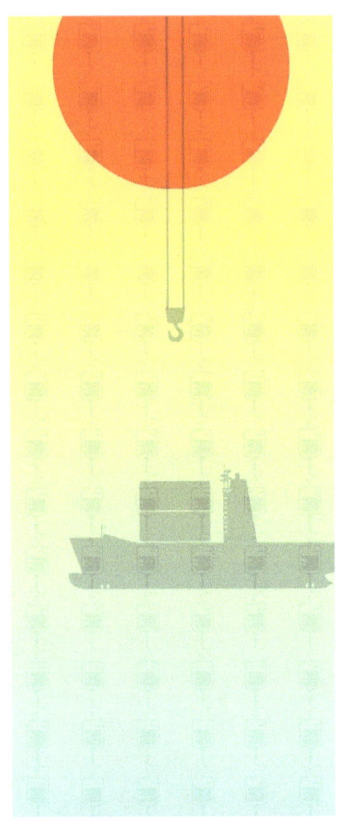
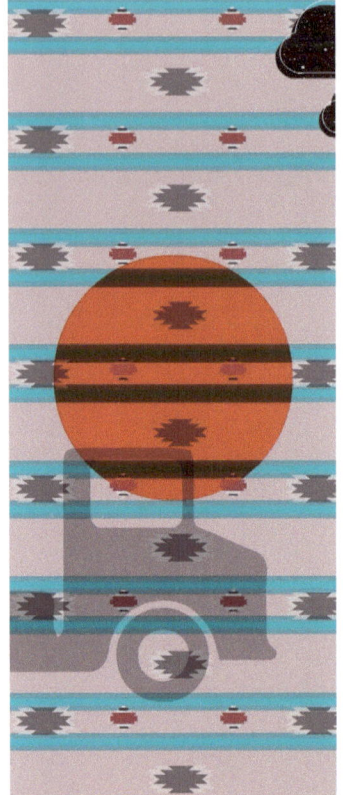
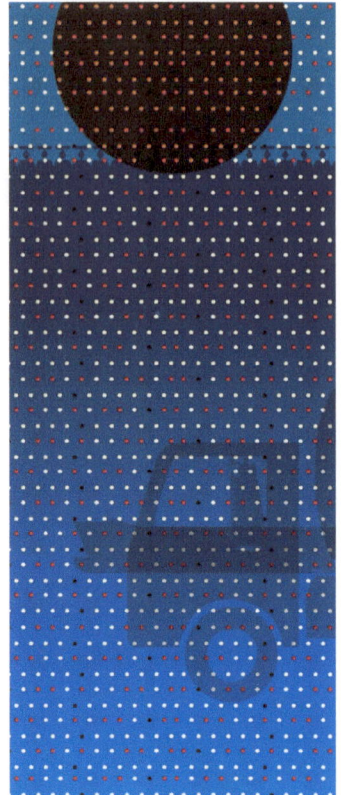
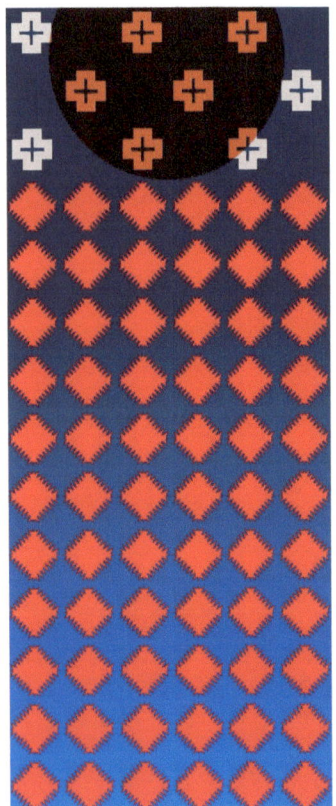
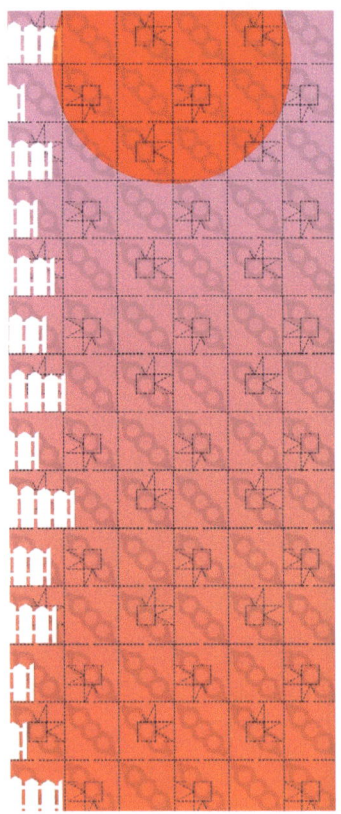
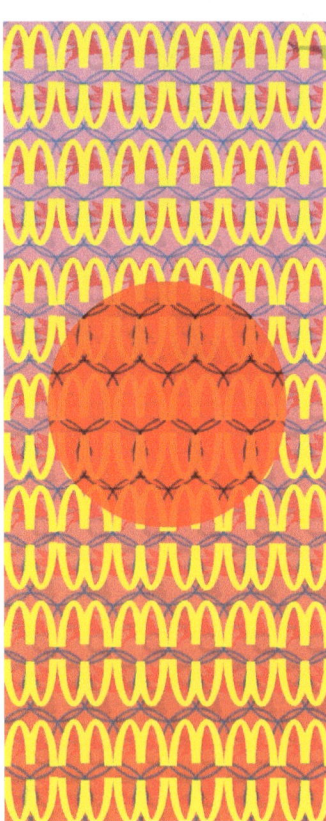

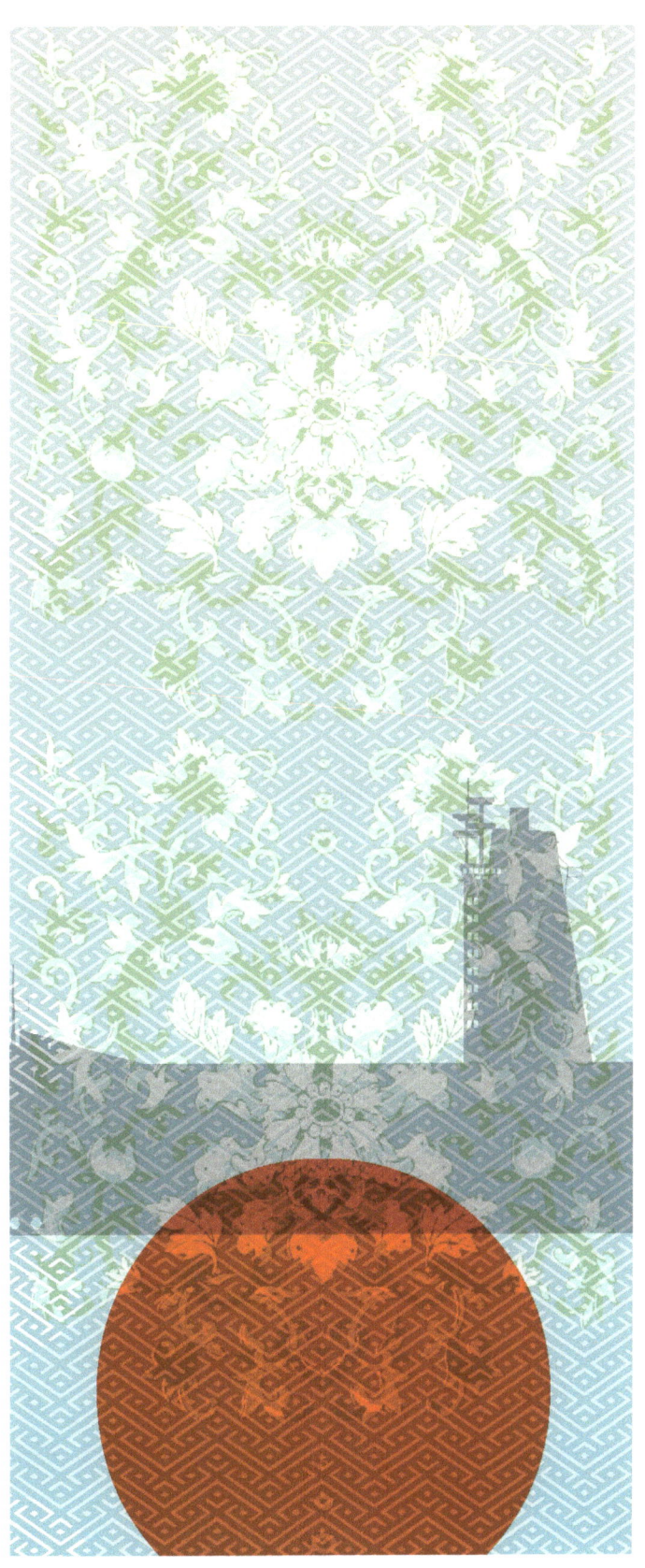

MORE&MORE (the invisible
oceans): United States (left)
and China (right)
Software driven animation
Color, sound
Dimensions variable
Edition of 3
2016

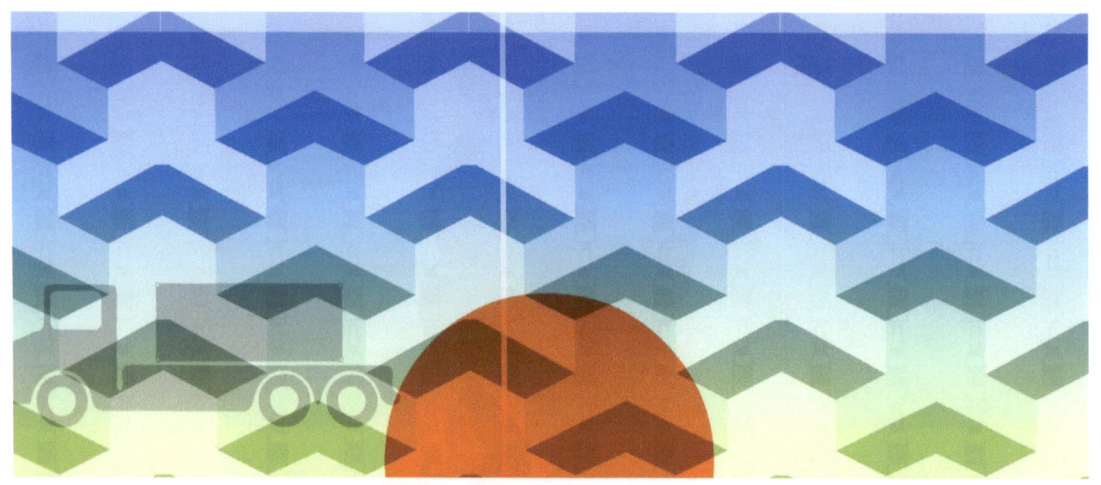

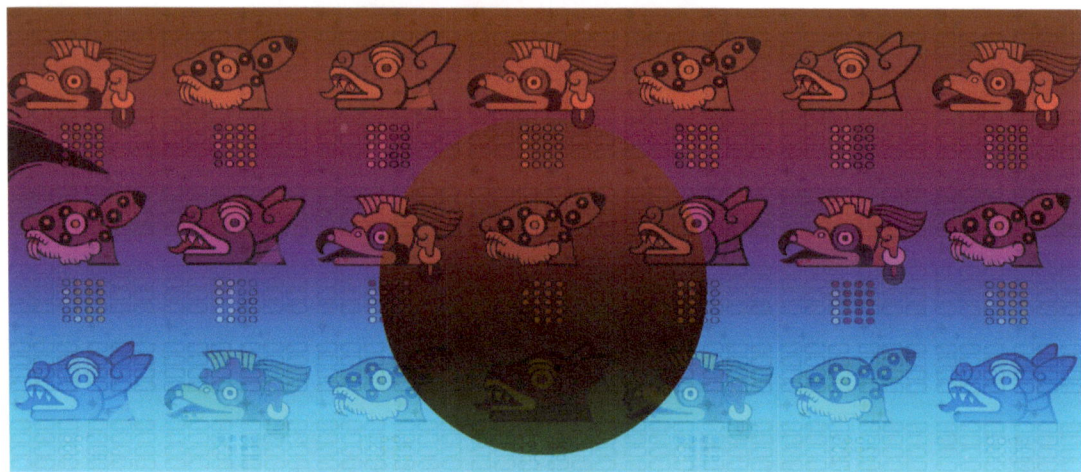

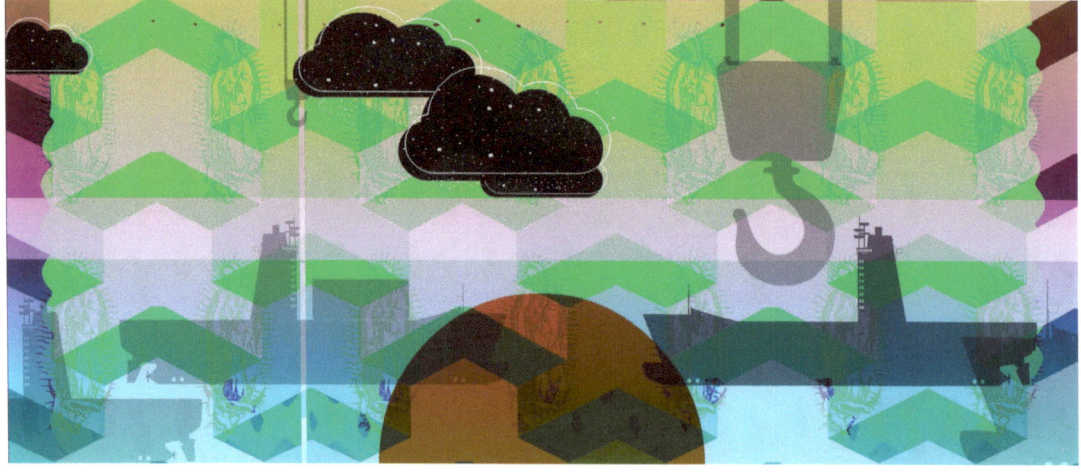

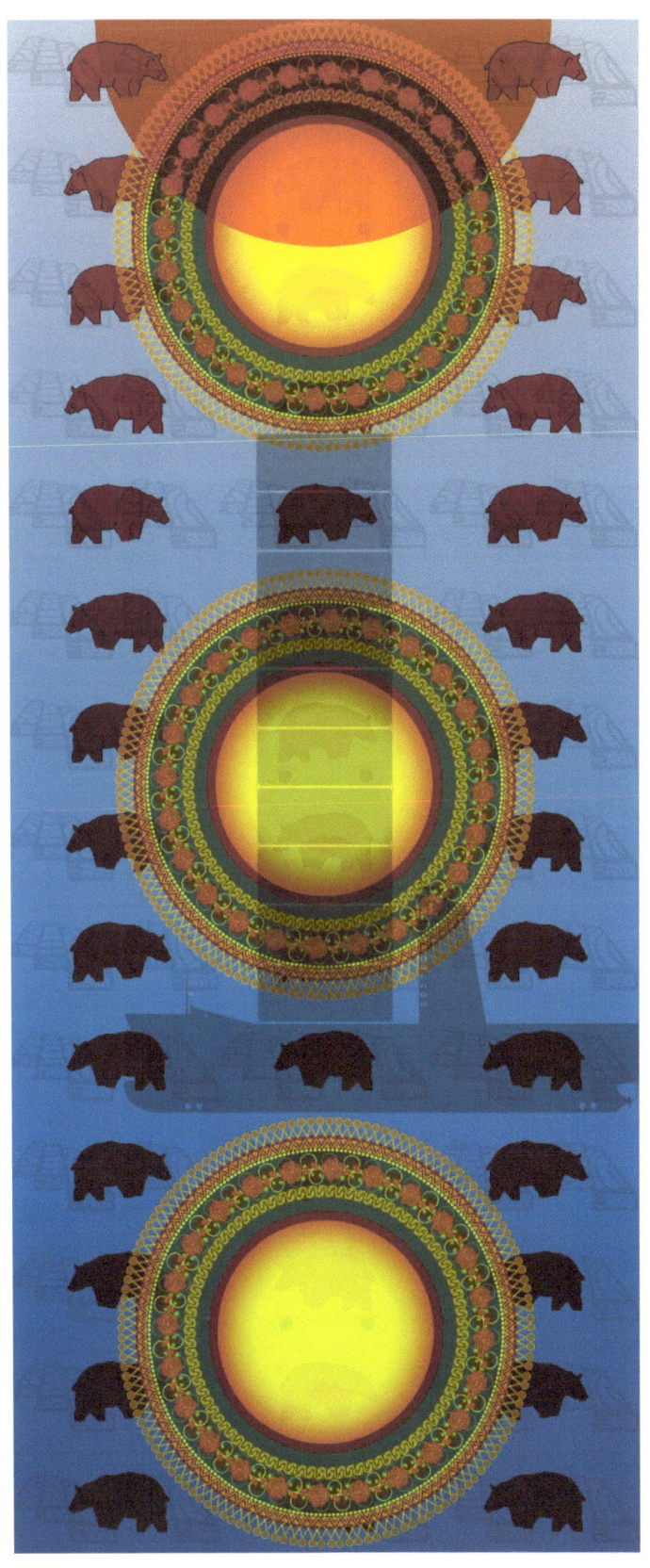

MORE&MORE (the invisible
oceans): Mexico (left) and
Russia (right)
Software driven animation
Color, sound
Dimensions variable
Edition of 3
2016

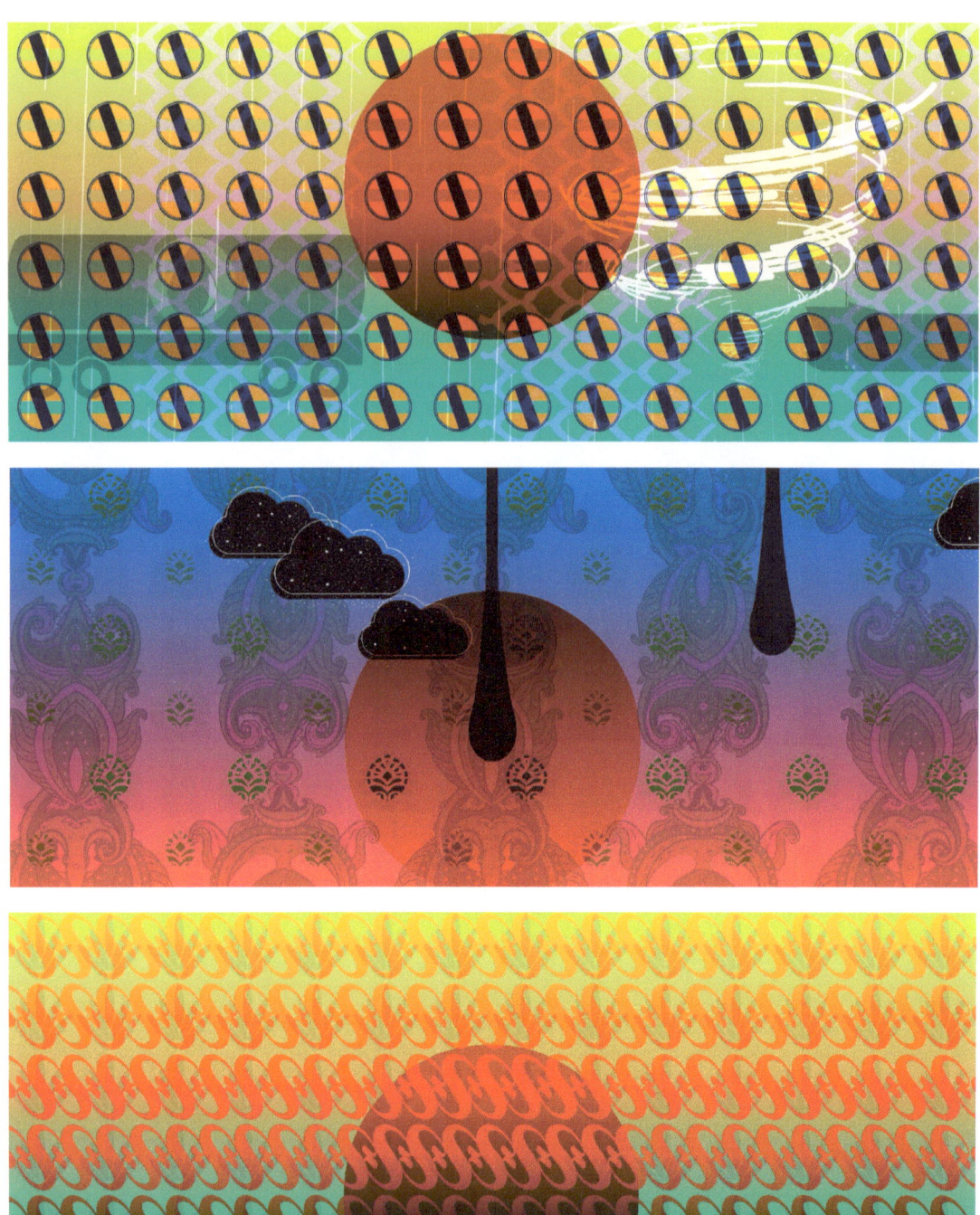

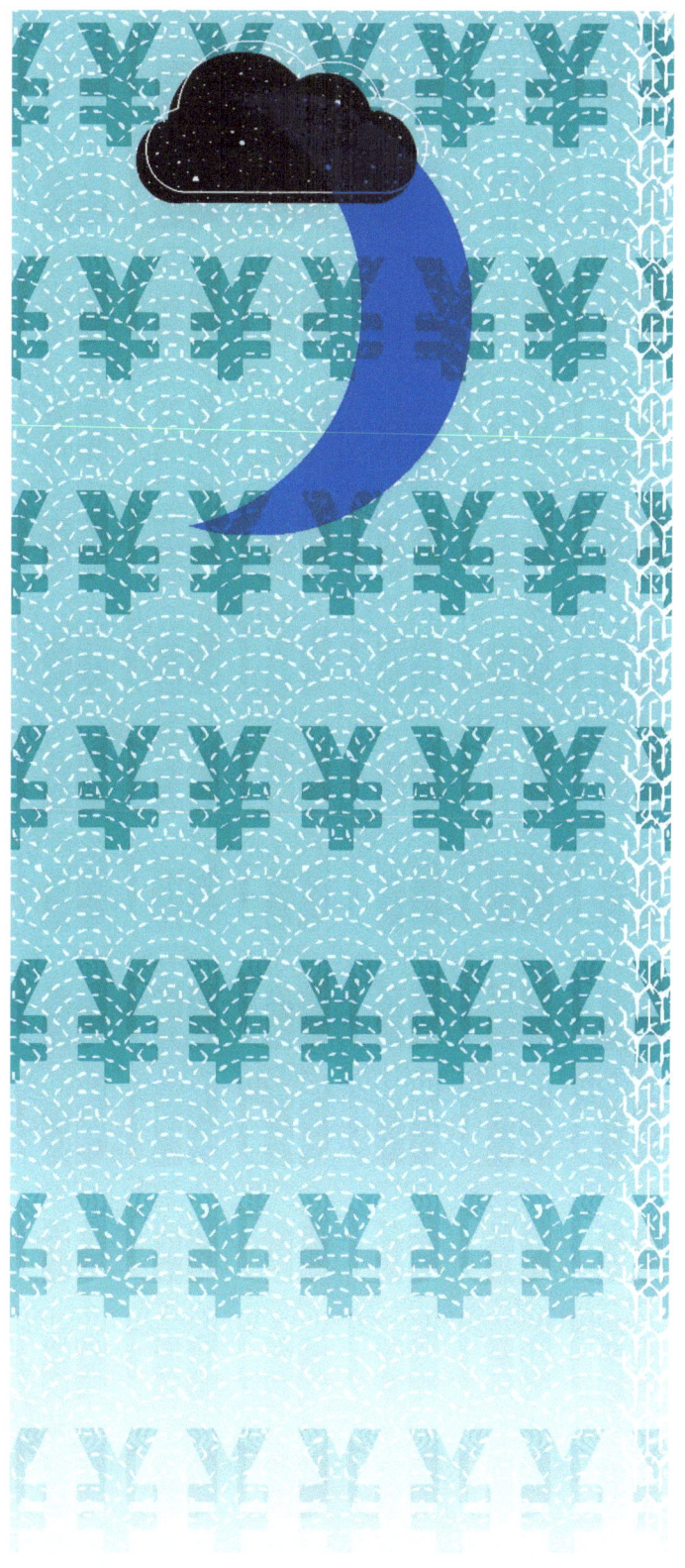

MORE&MORE (the invisible oceans):
India (left) and Japan (right)
Software driven animation
Color, sound
Dimensions variable
Edition of 3
2016

Nature is of course an elusive
category prone to slippage
between the material and the
divine, between substance and
essence...different kinds of
social organization produce wildly
different images of it. Nature is
for the moment then a category
without a content. It means simply
that which labor encounters.

— McKenzie Wark, *Molecular Red:
Theory for the Anthropocene*

The following conversation between Kathleen Forde, artistic director and cturator of Borusan Contemporary (Istanbul), and Marina Zurkow unfolded online in the months preceding the show.

KF There is a certain invisibility of the ocean, the sea, of water in this piece. And yet bodies of water are the overarching conduits of the shipping routes that you are exploring. Given that the nature and concerns of so much of your work is rooted in the ecological, I assume this void is clearly an intentional paradox?

MZ Yes. It's the void of the ocean...it's the ocean in the room...the liquid elephant in the room. How is it we can glide across it, plough through it, and close the gap between landmasses with a desire for the Pangaea made of capital? How can we forget, ignore or gloss over 78% of the earth's biosphere? Ultimately, I want to make work

Nature is of course an elusive category prone to slippage between the material and the divine, between substance and essence...different kinds of social organization produce wildly different images of it. Nature is for the moment then a category without a content. It means simply that which labor encounters.
– McKenzie Wark, _Molecular Red: Theory for the Anthropocene_

There are an estimated 30 million undiscovered species in the ocean but only 1.4 million known species on land. The largest animal communities on the planet and greatest number of individuals live below three thousand feet.
– James Nestor, _Deep: Freediving, Renegade Science, and What the Ocean Tells Us About Ourselves_

If you compare the ocean to a human body, the current exploration of the ocean is the equivalent of snapping a photograph of a finger to figure out how our bodies work. The liver, the stomach, the blood, the bones, the brain, the heart of the ocean – what's in it, how it functions, how we function within it – remain a secret, much of it hidden in the dark and sunless realms.
– James Nestor, _Deep: Freediving, Renegade Science, and What the Ocean Tells Us About Ourselves_

The ocean is a paradoxical space, both "capital's favored myth-element" and a site that suggests (unrealisable) potential for transcending its striations and structures.
– Phillip Steinberg, _Kimberley Peters Wet Ontologies_

about the ocean, in the ocean and for the ocean. But I have to admit that I got caught in the claustrophobic wonderland of the Harmonized System, of trade, and the absurd and/or upsetting density of it. This only serves to remind me that I too am a consumer, a human, dependent on these trade lines, and perhaps ignorant of supply chains.

KF We've referenced the Harmonized System a bunch in our conversations but I think it might be helpful to define what it is here as it is such an important structure for this project but not something I think many people (at least I was not) are familiar with.

MZ The Harmonized Commodity Description and Coding System (HS Code) is an internationally accepted standard of product classification, which codifies the way nations conduct import/export. All legal trade products (and illegal ones that find loopholes) are shipped using this system.

KF Can you explain a bit more by what you mean about forgetting the ocean? How is it getting forgotten and by whom?

MZ The ocean is, as Allan Sekula poignantly titled his film, a "Forgotten Space."

In no particular order: Maritime space is vast and ungovernable. Maritime law is broken all the time. International waters were an invention of the Dutch, in order to facilitate ocean trade in the early seventeenth century. For all of Grotius' ocean poetics, it ultimately was a play for global power through trade. The ocean is a slow feedback loop, and will, as a result of anthropogenic climatological changes, warm us for the next 50 years, whether we cease emitting CO_2 or not. It is on its own time scale. Ocean ecologies are relatively unknown, especially at depths greater than 2000 feet. Oceans are scary. We'd rather not think about their vastness. Despite their earthly dominance, we think about land. The Chinese are building islands to claim sovereignty over mineral and fishing rights in the ocean.

People swim near the shore, but, just as Deep Time is inconceivable on a daily basis, ocean depths are equally unimaginable — depths and landscapes more varied than the new mountains of Denali in Alaska, or the Himalayas.

KF How do you try to invert the invisibility of the ocean?

MZ In this installation and particularly in the animations, the ocean is in and out "there", we just don't see it in the animations. Ships skittering or gliding through space, as well as other means of transport like trucks, trains and planes but mostly ships and cranes placing and removing containers on ships. This is why we have bathing suits for people to buy in the space of the installation and online. So we can swim in *that* ocean.

KF In the animations we are looking at a selection of the highest volume port countries including India, USA, China, Japan, Turkey, Brazil, Russia and Mexico. The animations include representations of national identity associated with the port, the "happenings" of port life (cranes, trucks, ships), weather systems and indications of the passing of time. From what I understand, these are all being generated in real time. Are the real-time animations affected by live data? How does this strategy affect the viewer's experience of the work as opposed to a canned animation?

MZ The combinations of elements are generated in real time. The time of the port nation is set on the computer and dictates whether it is night or day. Because ports never close, there's not any need for marking time by month or special occasion. It is always on, always running. I could say there's no night or day too, but I wanted elements that marked time at its simplest. There is no real-time data.

Hopefully, the primary pleasure of the piece is one of pattern and decorative delirium — the patterns randomly combine, and there are about 50 patterns for each country. These now include icons for current trade export items, gas/bank/transport/telecom logos, as well as translations of decorative tiles and textiles

KF You've touched on the bathing suits above, but what about some of the other useless trade items rendered in fungus and chocolate evwaste. Can you fill me in a bit on your production and selection process?

As I'm sitting in this cramped metal sphere peering through the window at a seldom-seen habitat, I feel an emptiness in my chest that breath can't fill. This is the real Earth, the 71 percent silent majority. And this is how it looks — gelatinous, cross-eyed, clumsy, glowing, flickering, cloaked in perpetual darkness and compressed by more than a thousand pounds per square inch.
— *James Nestor, Deep: Freediving, Renegade Science, and What the Ocean Tells Us About Ourselves*

It takes a long time to become ooze. First you need to die and be eaten, then excreted, then have another organism eat that excrement, then have yet another animal eat that organism that just ate that excrement, and so on. This cycle will repeat until all that's left of you are a few million molecules spread out like a constellation of stars across the world's oceans.
— *James Nestor, Deep: Freediving, Renegade Science, and What the Ocean Tells Us About Ourselves*

It began to worry me, you see, this destruction of fish, this attrition of love that we were blindly bringing about, & I imagined a world of the future as a barren sameness in which everyone had gorged so much fish that no more remained, & where Science knew absolutely every species & phylum & genus, but no-one knew love because it had disappeared along with the fish.
— *Richard Flanagan, Gould's Book of Fish*

The sea's uses and moods sex it
— *John Fowles, Shipwreck*

Our species-being is as builders of worlds.
— *McKenzie Wark, Molecular Red: Theory for the Anthropocene*

The sea drowns the solid
outlines and protection of
modern technology and society
– Rose George, _Ninety Percent of_
Everything

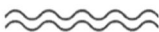

INFRASTRUCTURE

Photographer Allan Sekula, in
his book Fish Story, assaults
our intellectual reliance
upon an equivalence between
information and infrastructure:
"In effect, I am arguing for
the continued importance
of maritime space in order
to counter the exaggerated
importance attached to that
largely metaphysical construct,
"cyberspace," and the corollary
myth of "instantaneous"
contact between distance
spaces. I am often struck by
the ignorance of intellectuals
in this respect: the self-
congratulating conceptual
aggrandizement of "information"
frequently is accompanied by
peculiar erroneous beliefs:
among these is the widely held
quasi-anthropomorphic notion
that most of the world's
cargo travels as people do,
by air. This is an instance
of the blinkered narcissism
of the information specialist:
a "materialism" that goes no
farther than "the body."
– Adam Rothstein, _How to See_
Infrastructure: A Guide for Seven
Billion Primates, Rhizome.org

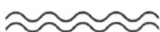

BLACK BOX

In science, computing, and
engineering, a black box is a
device, system or object which
can be viewed in terms of its
inputs and outputs (or transfer
characteristics), without any
knowledge of its internal
workings. Its implementation
is "opaque" (black). Almost
anything might be referred to
as a black box: a transistor,

MZ We (Surya Mattu and Sarah Rothberg and I) started
by analyzing the trade data based on the HS code (using
the Observatory of Economic Complexity API), and chose
several key recognizable items that represent the top export
items for a group of major port nations. For example, the
t-shirt, avocado, water bottle, mineral, computer, oil can,
frozen chicken, timber slice, revolution counter or diamond.

I made icons for the 1252 4-digit HS code categories,
and about 25 items we identified as key icons of illegally
transported and traded goods...from humans to rare
artifacts, to electronic waste to drugs.

We grew many of these iconic items out of fungus. Fungus
is a potential substitute for plastic – a chitinous, unlimited,
polymeric resource – that also speaks of death and decay.
Without fungus we'd all be miles and miles high in waste.
Plus fungi have survived 5 extinctions. Seemed pretty
robust.

The chocolate e-waste is still in progress. I have a lot of
strange chocolate molds purchased on the open market.
Computers and cell phones, edible sea life and beauty
accessories and tools and handcuffs. I am not sure yet if
we are going to make rarefied, anti-mass-scale commodity
consumables or highly shitty ones.

KF You have described this work as a new challenge to you
and a turning point in your practice, in what way?

MZ I have been critical of the fact that most of my previous
work neglected to address the social or economic. With this
project I have settled myself into a deep hole in which to
enjoy a steep learning curve by taking this issue on directly.

KF That's interesting to hear you say that. Personally,
I would not describe your previous work as neglecting
social content. Do you mean being more explicit about that
perspective in the work?

MZ One of the issues I have struggled with is a certain kind
of perceived misanthropy. I have focused on animals, plants,
weather – anthropogenic influences and the outcomes of
our complex systemic decisions. But when I speak about

ecological justice and the importance not only of a systems-level awareness, but also treating other species as equal to our own, I am often met with incredulity.

I have tried in this work to be more considered and inclusive of humans — not as villains or agents of the changes we so often are unwilling to look at on a systems level (unlimited growth, the mandate to scale up, the corporate bottom line, resource exploitation) — but rather as players, victims, animals, naturalized consumers who are completely distanced from how our consumption and its sources and effects are intertwined.

I should point out here that I am not excluding myself from this body of consumers. This endeavor is not an exorcism for me, nor a finger wagging excoriation of others. Once again, I am totally complicit, and it's a matter of coming-to-terms, or encountering intimately, the way I live.

My long-term goal with this project is to expand my thinking about capitalism as a delusional, untenable (land)mass, to find better-researched ways of working with this critique. And to advocate for human trafficking victims (so-called laborers, for instance) on the oceans, as well as the animals and plant life that are at risk because of the imperative to make and move STUFF at any cost from place to place.

KF The more I learn about the upcoming exhibition from you, the more it sounds like it functions more as an integrated installation, than a show of discreet works united by a common theme...does that ring true to you too?

MZ Yes; it's an additive process. I'm really focused on creating an experience of claustrophobia and delirium, useless empty commodities, absurd takes on cultural exports and on trade relations. Yet, I am looking at this from the perspective that they are still based on the reality of this system that depends on a certain kind of ignorance, or ignoring, I suppose. An ignoring of how, where, who and at what expense all of this shit is produced. At the same time I am focusing on the complex systemic outcomes that result from the production of stuff. My studio collaborators and myself are deliriously smitten with this — it's just incredible to us, still, after a year of work on this concept.

algorithm, or the human brain.
— Wikipedia

FLAGS OF CONVENIENCE

Flag of convenience is the business practice of registering a merchant ship in a sovereign state different from that of the ship's owners, and flying that state's civil ensign on the ship. Ships are registered under flags of convenience to reduce operating costs or avoid the regulations of the owner's country. The closely related term open registry is used to describe an organization that will register ships owned by foreign entities.

The term "flag of convenience" has been in use since the 1950s, and it refers to the civil ensign a ship flies in order to indicate its country of registration or flag state. A ship operates under the laws of its flag state, and these laws are used if the ship is involved in a case under admiralty law.

The modern practice of flagging ships in foreign countries began in the 1920s in the United States, when shipowners frustrated by increased regulations and rising labor costs began to register their ships to Panama. The use of open registries steadily increased, and in 1968, Liberia grew to surpass the United Kingdom as the world's largest shipping register. As of 2009, more than half of the world's merchant ships were registered with open registries, and the Panama, Liberia, and Marshall Islands flags accounted for almost 40% of the entire world fleet, in terms of deadweight tonnage.
— Wikipedia

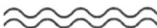

PRODUCTIVE KNOWLEDGE

Modern societies can amass
large amounts of productive
knowledge because they
distribute bits and pieces of
it among its many members.
But to make use of it, this
knowledge has to be put back
together through organizations
and markets. Our most
prosperous modern societies
are wiser, not because their
citizens are individually
brilliant, but because these
societies hold a diversity of
knowhow and because they are
able to recombine it to create
a larger variety of smarter and
better products.
– Hausmann, Hidalgo et al., *Atlas
of Economic Complexity*

ECONOMIC COMPLEXITY

How do we measure economic
complexity? The countries in
the top ten of this ranking are
Japan, Germany, Switzerland,
Sweden, Austria, Finland,
Singapore, Czech Republic, the
UK and Slovenia. Immediately
after the top 10 we have
France, Korea and the US. Of
the top 20 countries, half are
in Western Europe, 3 are in
East Asia, and surprisingly 4
are in Eastern Europe. Israel
and Mexico close the list of

We (Sarah and I) were also talking today at the studio about next steps for this work — and how we need to think about a counter-proposition: what if the containerization and transport was transparent, the process available, the materials open source?

KF When we met a few months ago you mentioned that you were going to be taking a journey yourself on a container ship from a port in China to the US. Which I didn't even know was "a thing" one could do. It's fascinating. Can you talk a little bit about what your intentions are for that journey and how it relates to this project?

MZ Sure, well to begin, Allan Sekula, the filmmaker I mentioned previously, was more concerned in his film with the forgotten neglected and exploited labor force of the seas in order for us get our stuff (merchant marines) but have never been celebrated and whose rights and honor have diminished greatly in the global economy. This is something that is of great importance to me too.

I am hoping to go to China by plane, wander around industrial and manufacturing cities, including older or even ancient ones and take a container ship back to the US. I want to be a thing amongst things on that ship. I have no idea what to expect — boredom, emptiness, nausea, nothing, whales, strangers, a jogging track, diesel fumes, a long drop from the deck to the sea, gigantic Terminator-like port machinery. A mid-sized ship is 10 blocks long. That is astonishing. 20 people work that ship. You eat with the captain and first mate. It is not glamorous.

It's tremendously important to me to do field work, to be in the field, for a length of time, upended, made strange. To have my biases contested by complex, often contradictory truths and a compassion for what is at hand. Things like people, biases other than my own, social and biological systemic co-dependencies, and the always-surprising affordances of the landscape when you encounter it in person and let it slowly enfold and influence you.

the top 20. These are countries with productive structures that are able to hold vast amounts of productive knowledge, and that manufacture and export a large number of sophisticated goods. At the bottom of the economic complexity ranking we have Papua New Guinea.
The Republic of Congo, Sudan, Angola and Mauritania.
– *Hausmann, Hidalgo et al.*, *Atlas of Economic Complexity*

Each container is accompanied by a manifest listing its contents, but neither ship lines nor ports can vouch that what is on the manifest corresponds to what is inside. Nor is there any easy way to check: opening the doors at the end of the box normally reveals only a wall of paperboard cartons. With a single ship able to disgorge 3,000 40-foot-long containers in a matter of hours, and with a port such as Long Beach or Tokyo handling perhaps 10,000 loaded containers on the average workday, and with each container itself holding row after row of boxes stacked floor to ceiling, not even the most careful examiners have a remote prospect of inspecting it all. Containers can be just as efficient for smuggling undeclared merchandise, illegal drugs, undocumented immigrants, and terrorist bombs as for moving legitimate cargo.
– *Marc Levinson*, *The Box: How the Shipping Container Made the World Smaller and the World Economy Bigger*

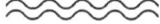

CARGO

Allan Sekula, in his book Fish Story, writes about Michel Foucault's definition of a heterotopia, a displacement habitat, a place that exists between places. Cemeteries, fairgrounds, retirement homes, psychiatric hospitals. But the best heterotopia, he writes, is the ship, "a floating piece of space, a place without a place, that exists by itself, that is closed in on itself and at the same time is given over to the infinity of the sea."
– *Rose George*, *Ninety Percent of Everything*

...the largest man-made moving objects on the planet.
– *Rose George*, *Ninety Percent of Everything*

Affixed to an image of shipping containers which we might surmise contain the components of the export of the Western beauty myth (be these cosmetics, domestic appliances, or indeed the military ordnance needed to "open doors" to US capital), the term cargo cult of course echoes the anthropological inversion already at work in the history of the idea of commodity fetishism – beauty under capital is a monetised social relation between things, just as the beauty industry is in turn an irrational, ritualised invocation of future "cargo".
– *Kinkle and Toscano*, *Cartographies of the Absolute*

The biggest container ship can carry fifteen thousand boxes. It can hold 746 million bananas, one for every European on one ship. If the containers of Maersk alone were lined up, they would stretch eleven thousand miles or nearly halfway around the planet. If they were stacked instead, they would be fifteen hundred miles high, 7,530 Eiffel Towers. If Kendal discharged her containers onto trucks, the line of traffic would be sixty miles long.
– *Rose George*, *Ninety Percent of Everything*

Shipping is so cheap that it makes more financial sense for Scottish cod to be sent ten thousand miles to China to be filleted, then sent back to Scottish shops and restaurants, than to pay Scottish filleters. A Scottish newspaper called this practice "madness," but actually it's just shipping.
– *Rose George*, *Ninety Percent of Everything*

Container manifests rely on the legal term "said to contain." Security people will assure you that intelligence and clever analysis can fill in the rest of the percentages, that they can spot smuggled goods, people, or weapons... All sorts of criminals like ships. Counterfeiters ship $200 billion worth of fake goods in them, or more than the GDP of 150 countries. People traffickers regularly send their desperate clients off in boxes. Drug barons love boxes. In one report, the GAO was blunt: "U.S. initiatives relating to cargo container security have been limited and generally ineffective for the international counter narcotics effort."
– *Rose George*, *Ninety Percent of Everything*

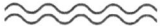

LABOR

The Scythian philosopher Anacharsis was once asked whether there were more people alive or dead. He couldn't answer, said Anacharsis, because he didn't know where to place seamen. "Seamen," concluded the seventeenth-century clergyman John Flavel, who quotes this remark, "are, as it were, a third sort of persons, to be numbered neither

with the living nor the dead;
their lives hanging continually
in suspense before them."
— *Rose George, <u>Ninety Percent of
Everything</u>*

Two thousand seafarers die at
sea every year...more than two
ships are lost every week.
— *Rose George, <u>Ninety Percent of
Everything</u>*

Buy your fair-trade coffee
beans by all means, but don't
assume fair-trade principles
govern the conditions of the
men who fetch it to you.
— *Rose George, <u>Ninety Percent of
Everything</u>*

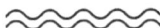

TRASH AND CAPITAL

The tourists had insistent,
unspoken questions and we
just had to answer as best we
could, with forged furniture.
They were really asking, 'Are
we safe?' and we were really
replying, 'No, but a barricade
of useless goods may help block
the view.'
— *Richard Flanagan, <u>Gould's Book
of Fish</u>*

The massive plastic trash gyre
isn't an island, it's the
disaster of capital circling
the globe on ocean currents.
...what breaks down doesn't
remain solely in the Garbage
Patch; that anywhere ocean
currents converge is this
toxic soup. That this soup is
suffused with Bisphenol A,
phthalates, polychlorinated
biphenyls, persistent organic
pollutants, and other
remainders from discarded
commodities that contribute
directly to the ocean
acidification killing fragile
ecosystems.

Under this system, the
overwhelming majority of

goods that make convenient
consumer culture possible are
composed of manmade polymers,
including but not limited to
whiskey bottles, water and soda
bottles, bottle caps, six-pack
loops, industrial felt, fishing
rope, nylon flags, fleece
sweaters, shoes, purses, eating
utensils, cups, bowls, cell
phones, computers, printers,
furniture, toys, and, of
course, plastic bags.
— *Maya Weeks, <u>Myth of the Garbage
Patch</u>*

How do we pollute the ocean?
With plastic and chemicals and
sewage, but also with noise...
The movement of propellers in
water produces something known
as cavitation: a constant
creation of tiny bubbles that
constantly pop. Aquatic bubble
wrap. The cavitation of a
freighter leaving Cape Cod
Canal can be heard all over the
bay. A supertanker can be heard
in the sea a day before its
arrival...Researchers had been
looking at daily, weekly, or
monthly noise rates.

When they compared levels
over a longer timescale, the
results were shocking. Ambient
noise in the deep ocean was
increasing by 3 decibels every
decade. Every ten years, noise
from commercial shipping had
doubled...Sonar, pinging,
and air guns are intense but
discrete and short-lived.
Shipping noise is always
there. Christopher Clark, a
Cornell University professor
and acoustic specialist, calls
commercial shipping "by far the
most ubiquitous anthropogenic
contributor to ocean noise."
Humpback whales now have 10
percent of the acoustic range
they used to have, so that
their chances of finding a
mate, food, and probably
surviving have all been
decimated.
— *Rose George, <u>Ninety Percent of
Everything</u>*

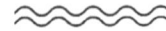

KF Are there essays texts
or books that affected your
thinking about this work?

MZ Rose George, 90% of
Everything
Ian Urbina's NY Times series
"Outlaw Ocean"
Marc Levinson The Box: How the
Shipping Container Made the
World Smaller
Phil Steinberg The Social
Construction of the Ocean
Stacy Alaimo's work, esp the
essay Violet Black

KF Documentaries?

MZ Alan Sekula, "The Forgotten
Space"

KF Web sites (project related)

MZ Observatory of Economic
Complexity
The idea of "productive
knowledge"

KF An event, trip, residency
etc that has most inspired your
practice/this show in 2015?

MZ This show was triggered
by the animated piece
"Mesocosmico: Paulista" that I
did with Sarah Rothberg for São
Paulo in 2014. We had a very
short turnaround time to make
a work for a 20 story building
on the main shopping street
in São Paulo for a week-long
outdoor screening festival
called SP Urban. The pixel size
of the building was minuscule,
and it forced me to reconsider
my aesthetic approach. I was
interested in making something
that would not feel like an
ad, or a decoration, and we
landed on a treatment of a
software-driven work that took

key endangered endemic species
of animal and tree from the
disappearing forest of the
state of São Paulo called the
Atlantic Rainforest of Brazil,
and combining this with visual
patterns that defined São
Paolo (such as the cobblestone
street patterns). This led to a
consideration of what cultural
exports look like, and how
influenced by early global
trade they really are.

KF Art/artist?

MZ Unknown Fields
Phil Ross, my mentor in fungus

KF Most influential / favorite
artists not necessarily
related to this project / life
in general)

MZ Artists I think about and
am inspired by:
General: Peter Breughel
the Elder and Wang Hui
for their works' density,
unrealism, attention to
detail and allegory. Dieter
Roth, Rosemary Trockel, Kiki
Smith, Marcus Coates, Saul
Bass, film titles from the
50s/60s, elBulli Restaurant,
Mark Lombardi, Morgan Puett,
Walid Raad, Spencer Finch,
Tim Hawkinson, Philip Guston,
Sue Williams, Robert Smithson,
the Situationists, writers
Timothy Morton (The Ecological
Thought), Jane Bennett (Vibrant
Matter and The Enchantment of
Modern Life), Una Chaudhuri,
Michael Pollan (Botany of
Desire)

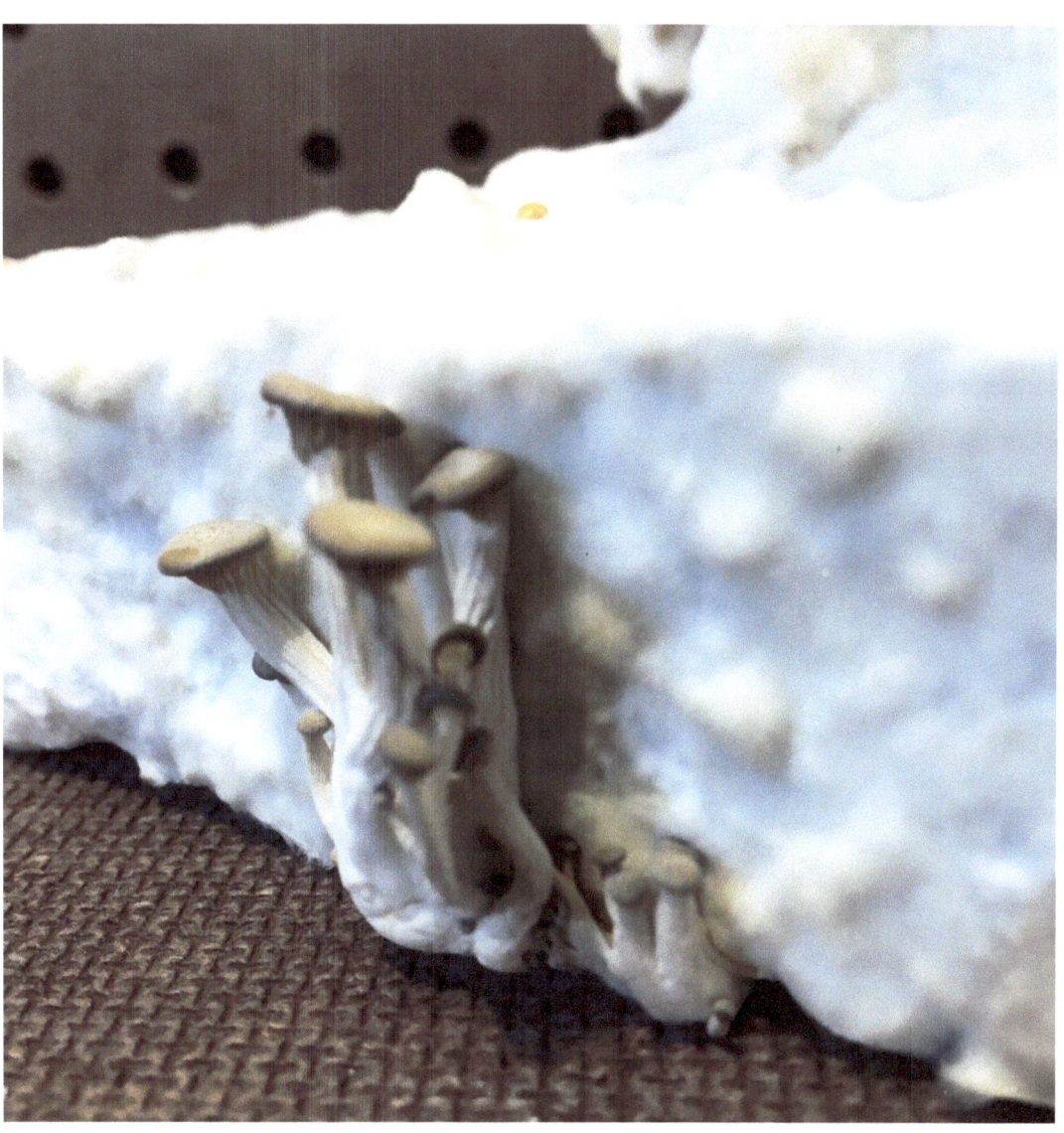

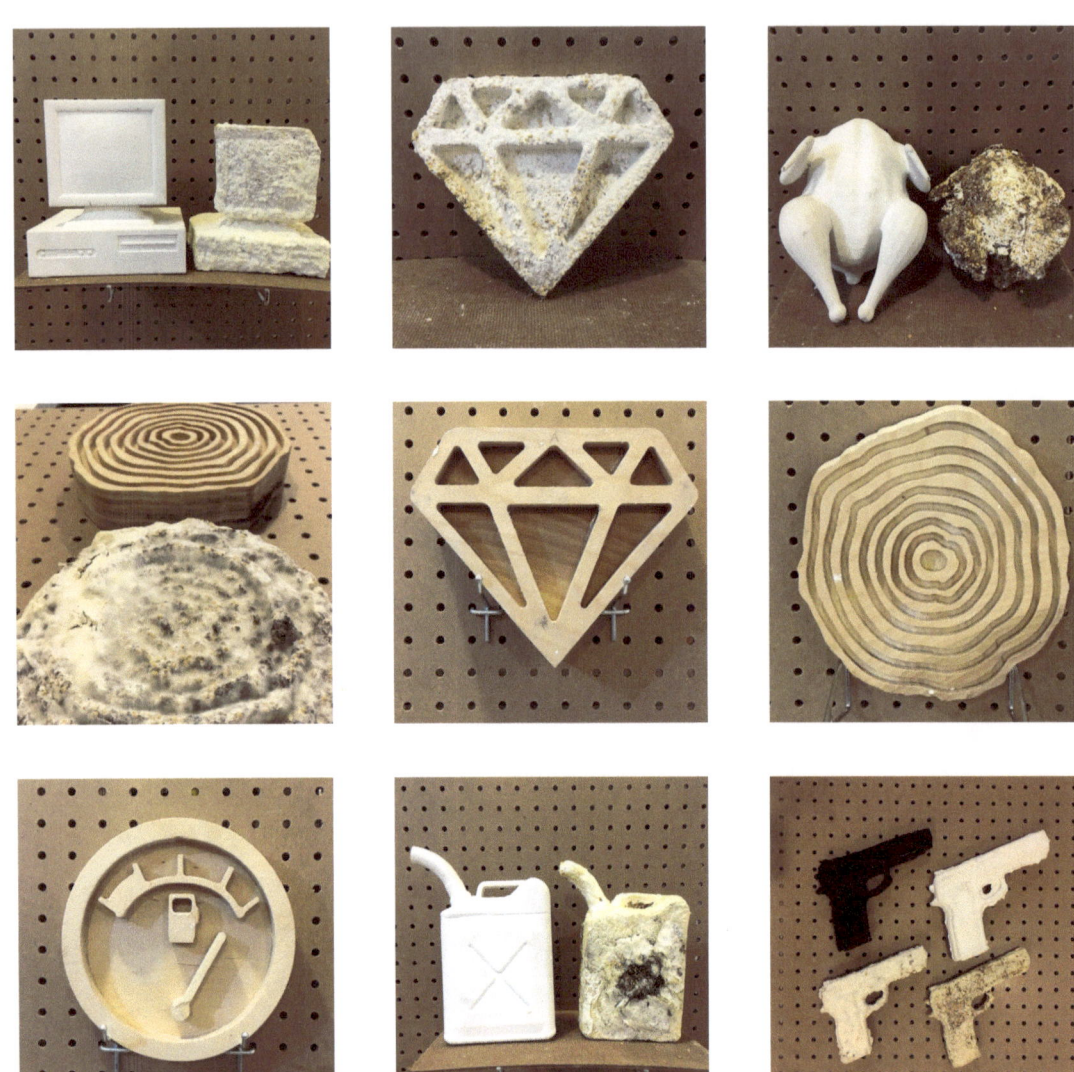

More&More Shop Products
3D powder, plaster, wood, fungus,
coffee husks
Approx 8" x 8"
Unique objects
2016

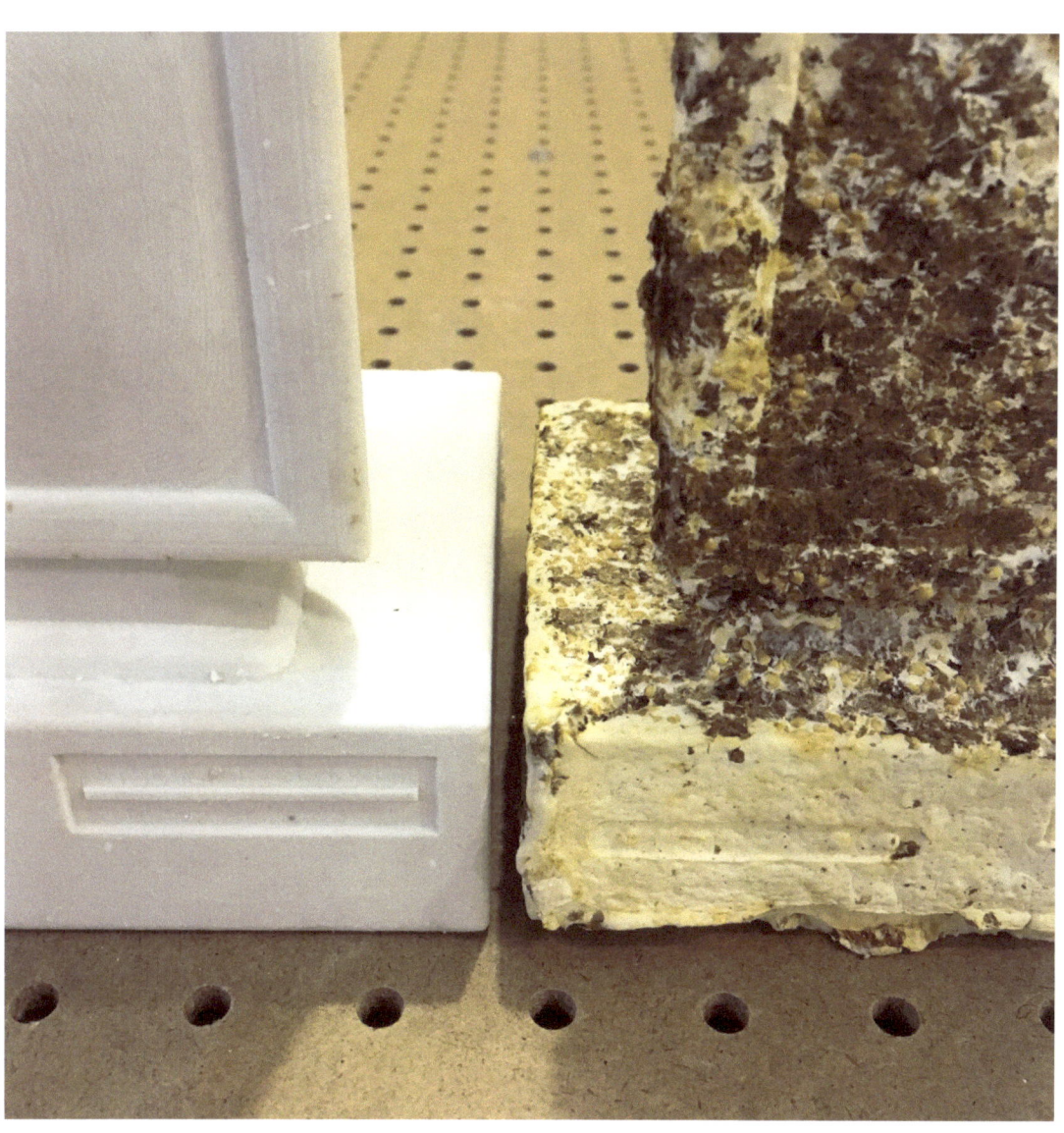

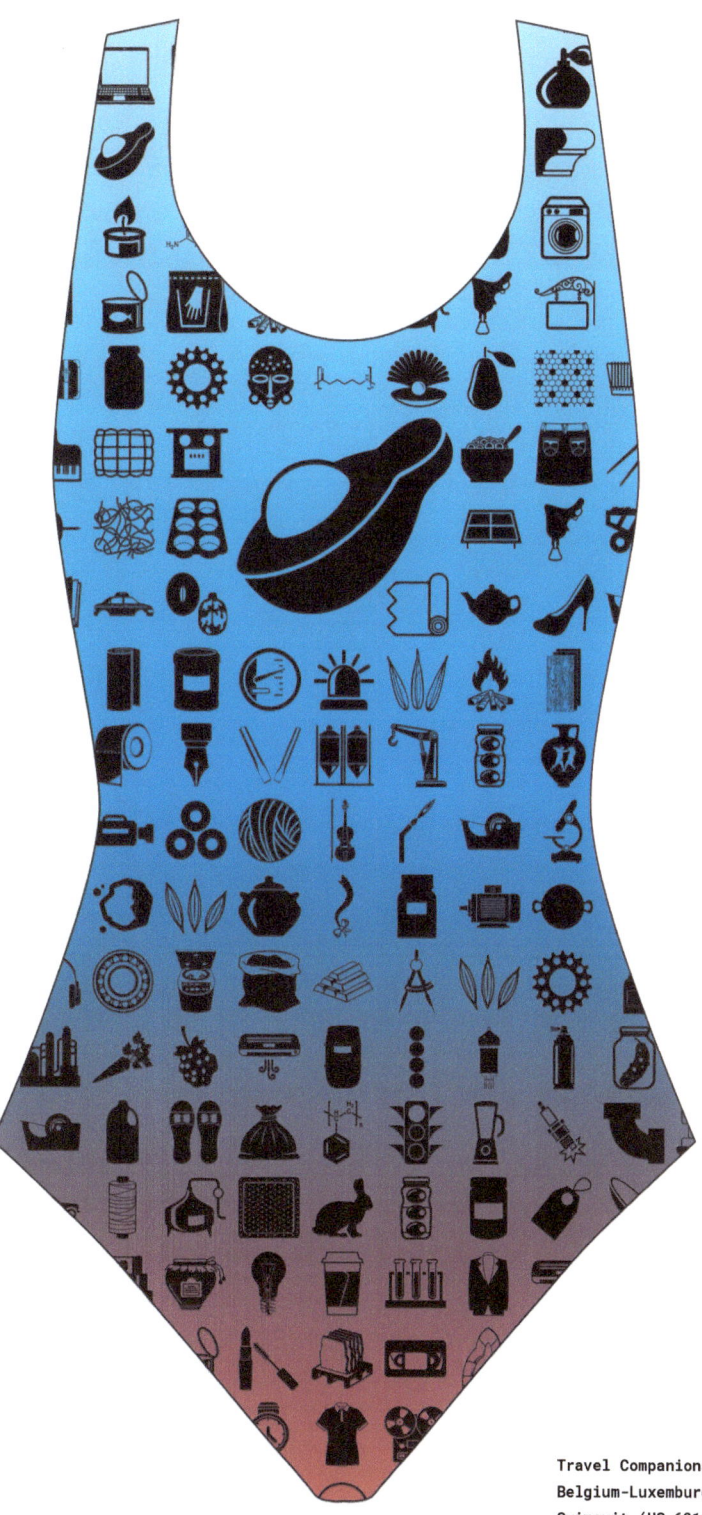

Travel Companions for a Diamond from
Belgium-Luxemburg to India, 2016
Swimsuit (HS 62112)
Unique, print on demand bathing suits
Custom-ordered through moreandmore.world
and made by Print All Over Me

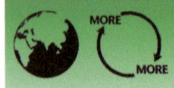

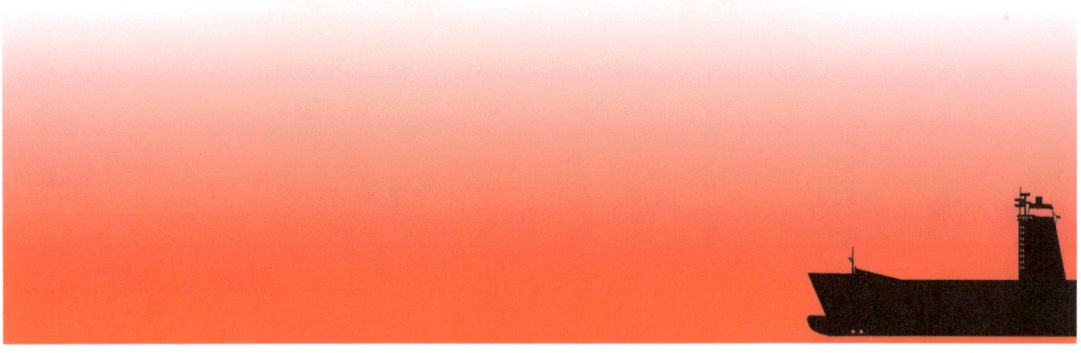

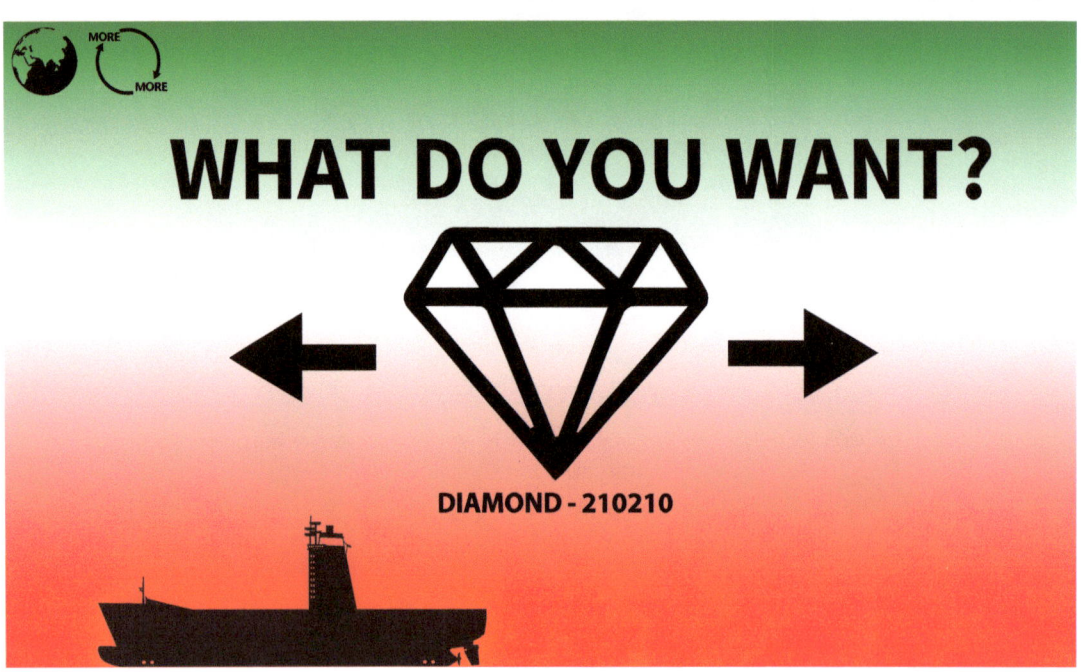

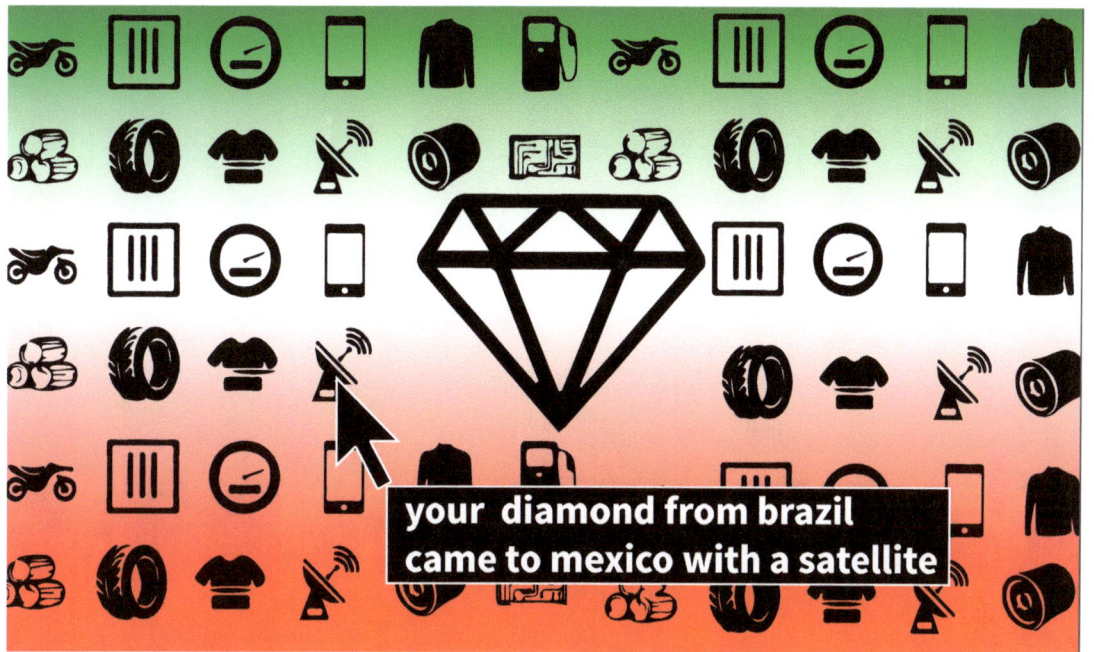

your diamond from brazil
came to mexico with a satellite

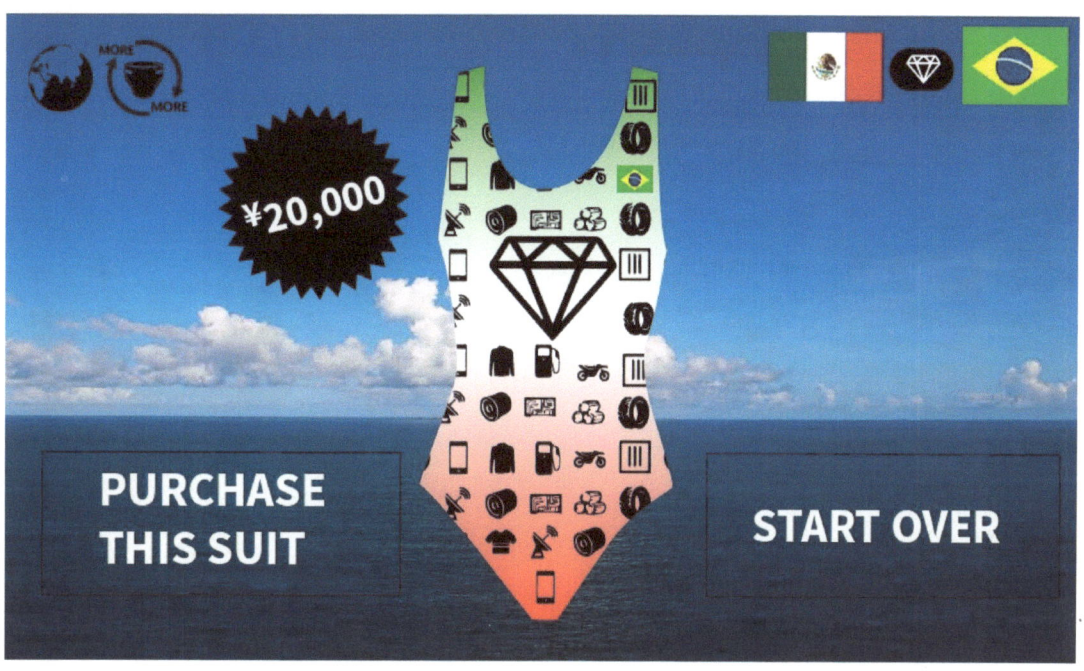

¥20,000

PURCHASE
THIS SUIT

START OVER

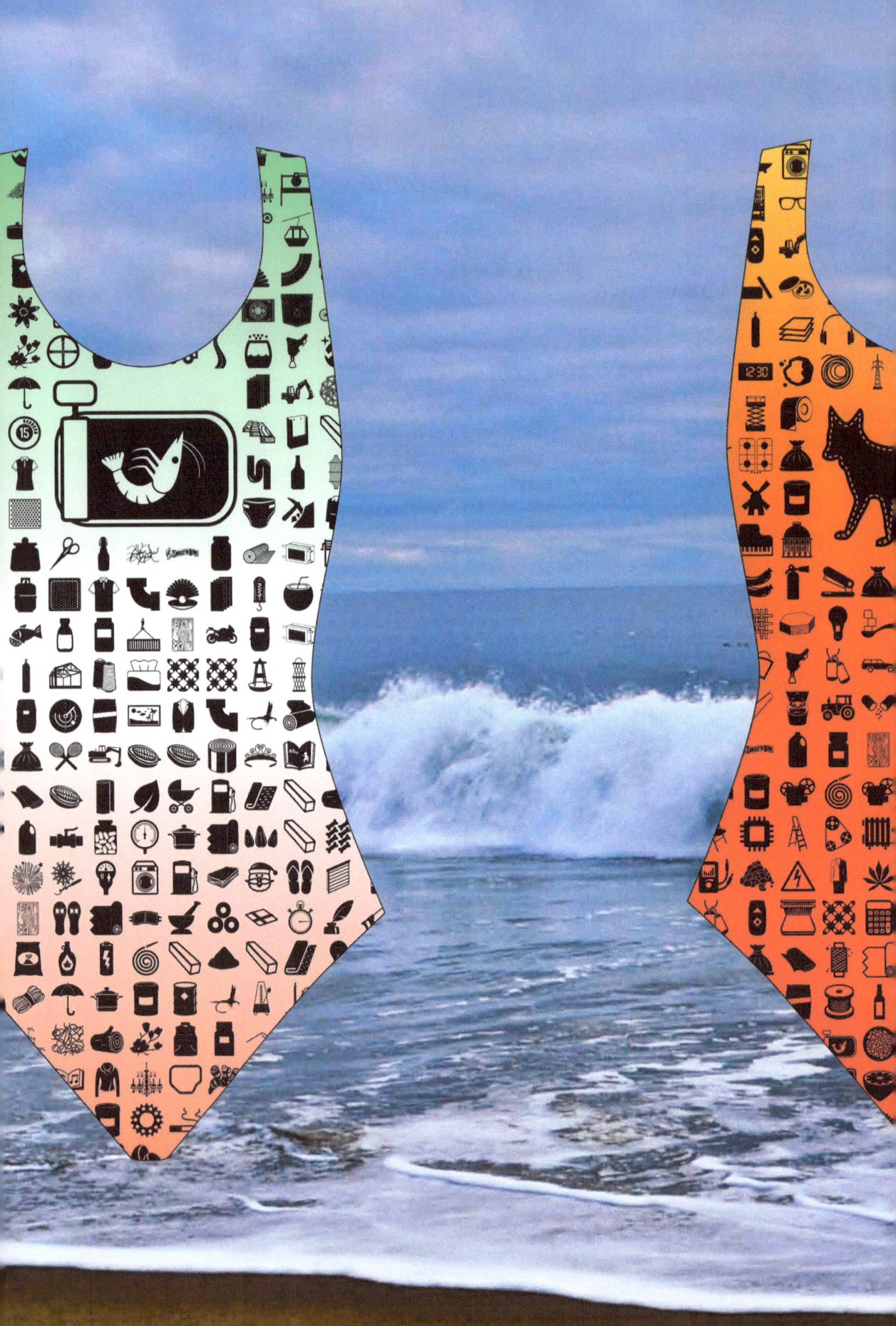

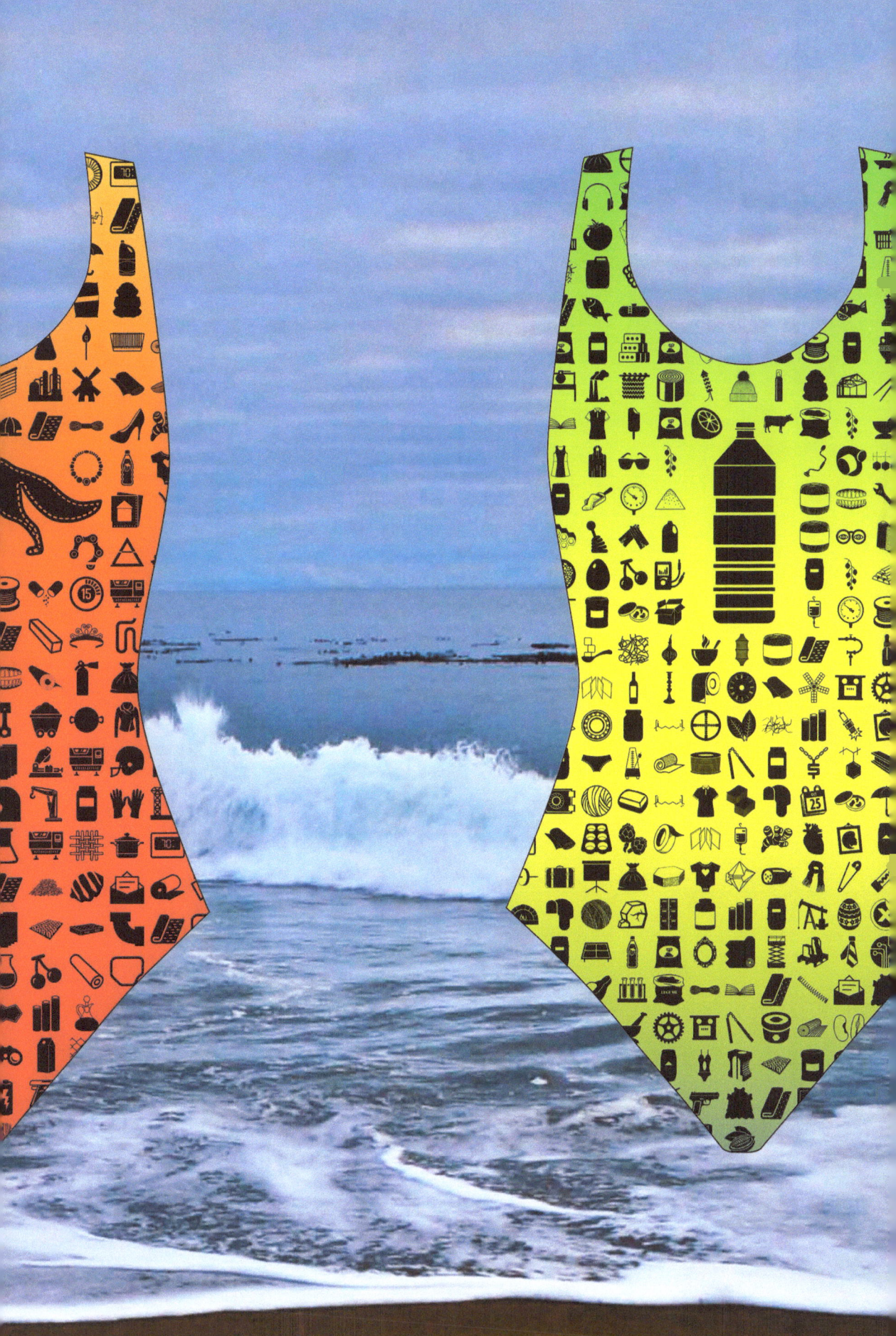

HISTORY OF GLOBAL TRADE
http://tinyurl.com/74l6hja

OPEN DATA ON IMPORT/EXPORT

The Observatory of Economic
Complexity: OEC
atlas.media.mit.edu/

MARINE TRAFFIC MONITORING
http://www.marinetraffic.com/

INTERNATIONAL MARITIME
ORGANIZATION DATABASE
https://gisis.imo.org/Public/
Default.aspx

"HOW TO EXPORT IMPORT"

A breakdown of what kinds of
products are listed in the HS Code
http://howtoexportimport.com/
Harmonized-System-Codes-HS-codes-
Chapter-01-to-97-811.aspx

How to start a container ship
business
http://tinyurl.com/jy6g4z5

BUSIEST PORTS
http://en.wikipedia.org/wiki/
List_of_world%27s_busiest_
container_ports

PORT INDUSTRY STATISTICS
http://www.aapa-ports.org/
Industry/content.cfm?Item
Number=900&navItemNumber=551

ECOPORTS
http://www.ecoports.com/

PORTS CLIMATE INITIATIVE
http://wpci.iaphworldports.org/
project-in-progress/index.html

FLAGS OF (IN)CONVENIENCE
http://www.economist.com/news/
business/21602237-flags-
inconvenience

PIRACY
Real-time piracy map
https://icc-ccs.org/piracy-
reporting-centre/live-piracy-map

Piracy Incidents reports
https://gisis.imo.org/Public/PAR/
Default.aspx

ILLEGAL TRAFFICKING OVERVIEW
http://www.worldwatch.org/node/523

Map of Illegal Trade Routes
http://www.substance.com/map-the-
worlds-illegal-trade-routes/16547/

Interpol
http://www.interpol.int/INTER-
POL-expertise/Databases

Interpol Casebook
http://tinyurl.com/j6hav8a

Bureau of Foreign Trade
http://cus93.trade.gov.tw/ENGLISH/
FSCE/

Stockholm International Peace
Research Institute
http://tinyurl.com/gmwqty7

ARMS
http://geographicalimaginations.
com/2012/08/08/the-death-
merchants/
http://www.armsflow.org/
https://arirusila.wordpress.com/
tag/arms-trade/
http://www.dataviva.info/profiles/
hs/19/?app=1
http://nisat.prio.org/Data-
Visualization/

GLOBAL WASTE TRADE POLICIES
http://toxicslink.org/?q=
policiesinternational

The Basel Action Network
http://www.ban.org/

Illegal Flows Map
http://worldloop.org/e-waste/
illegal-flows/

Transboundary Waste Shipments
http://leon.creait.mun.ca/
ewaste-export/networks/2012/index.
html

Visualizing Waste
http://scalar.usc.edu/works/
reassembling-rubbish/visualiz-
ing-transboundary-
shipments-of-e-waste

Global E-Waste Monitor
http://tinyurl.com/j2r3w7b

Waste Crime, Waste Risks
http://tinyurl.com/j5pczwm

Global Review of Waste Management
http://tinyurl.com/74x6p6u

Tracking the Global Generation and
Exports of e-Waste
http://pubs.acs.org/doi/
abs/10.1021/es5021313

DRUGS

CIA factbook
https://www.cia.gov/Library/
publications/the-world-factbook/
fields/2086.html

World Drug Report
http://www.unodc.org/wdr2015/

HUMAN TRAFFICKING
http://humantraffickingcenter.
org/posts-by-htc-associates/memex-
helps-find-human-
trafficking-cases-online/
http://www.unodc.org/unodc/en/
data-and-analysis/glotip.html

ENDANGERED SPECIES
CONVENTION ON INTERNATIONAL
TRADE IN ENDANGERED SPECIES
http://trade.cites.org/

Endangered Species Databases
http://www.earthsendangered.com/
search-regions3.asp
http://www.animalinfo.org/
http://www.iucnredlist.org/about/
summary-statistics
http://europe.chinadaily.com.cn/
epaper/2014-02/14/
content_17282358.htm
https://occrp.org/occrp/en/inves-
tigations/2596-
endangered-animals-enter-
armeniaand-then-go-where

ARTIFACTS
http://www.unesco.org/new/en/cul-
ture/themes/illicit-
trafficking-of-cultural-property/
databases/
https://www0.gsb.columbia.edu/
faculty/rfisman/papers/
artsmuggling.pdf
http://www.interpol.int/notice/
search/woa

JELLYFISH WATCH LIST
http://www.jellywatch.org/
sightings_list

FISHING/OVERFISHING
COMMERCIAL FISHERIES STATISTICS
http://tinyurl.com/hybqcr7
http://www.fishwatch.gov/
http://www.seafoodwatch.org/

Big data allow fish to be
protected as never before.
Governments should take advantage
of this
http://tinyurl.com/krvuuws

DEEP SEA CAMS
http://www.oceannetworks.ca/
sights-sounds/video/live-video/
tempo-mini-vent-camera
http://www.nautiluslive.org/
http://oceanexplorer.noaa.gov/
okeanos/media/exstream/exstream.
html

ARTISTS

Unknown Fields
http://www.unknownfieldsdivision.
com/winter2013china-aworld
adriftpart01.html
http://www.unknownfieldsdivision.
com/summer2014china-aworld
adriftpart02.html

Phil Ross
http://philross.org/

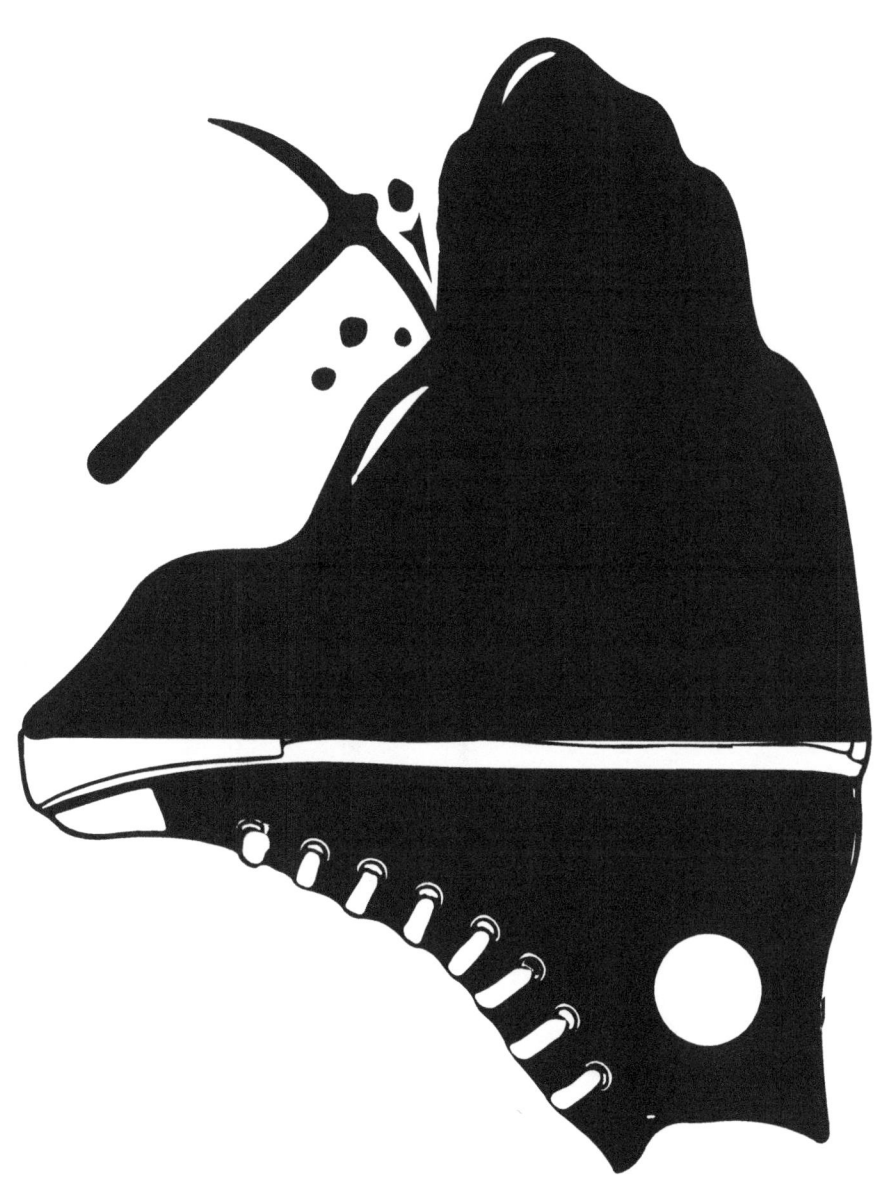

Untitled Drawings
2016

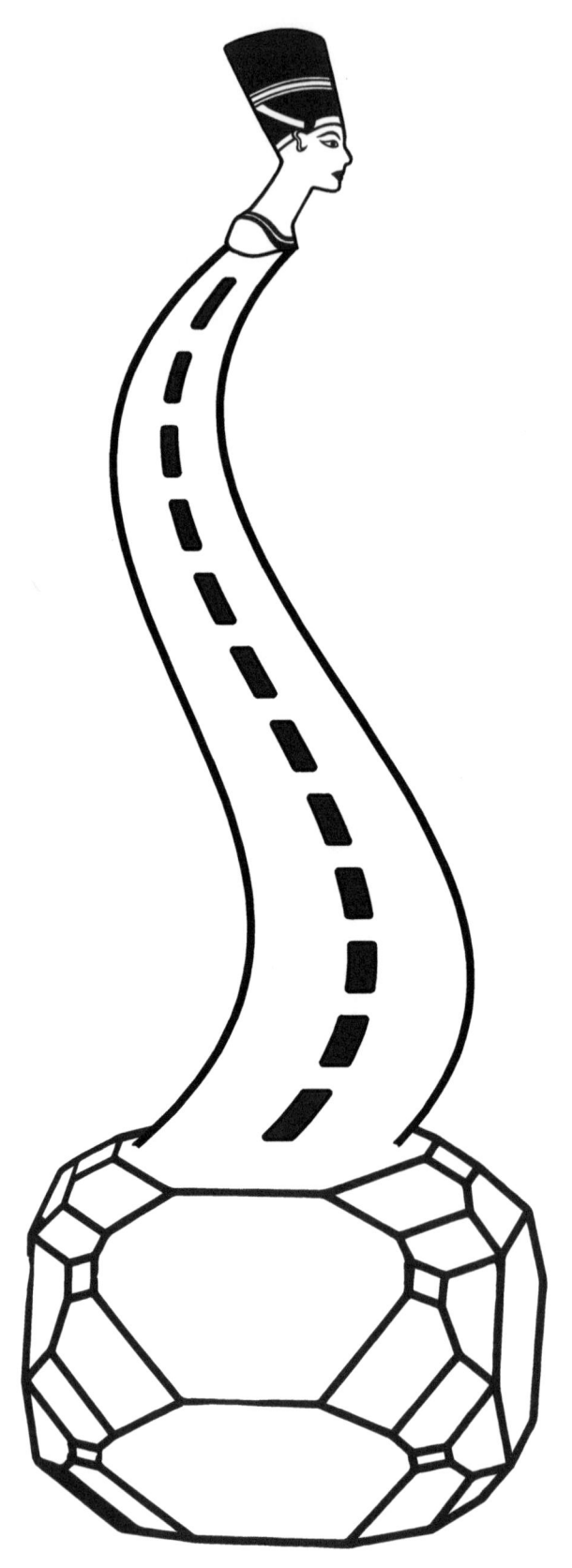

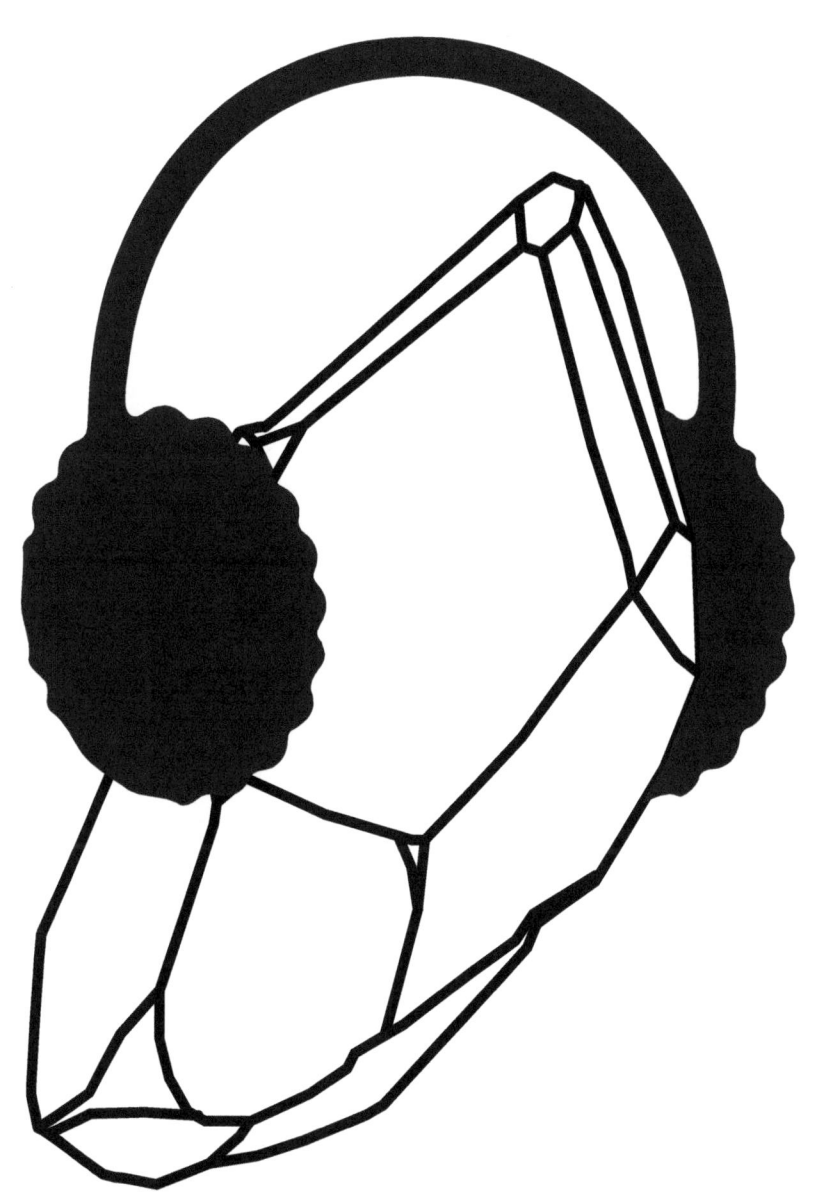

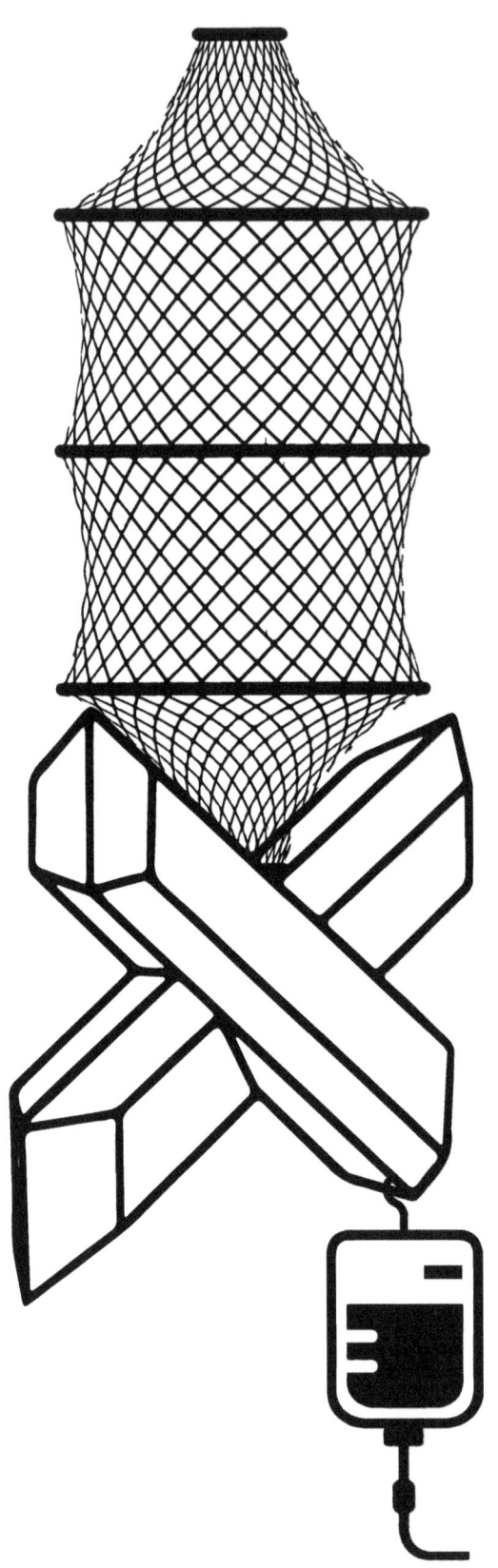

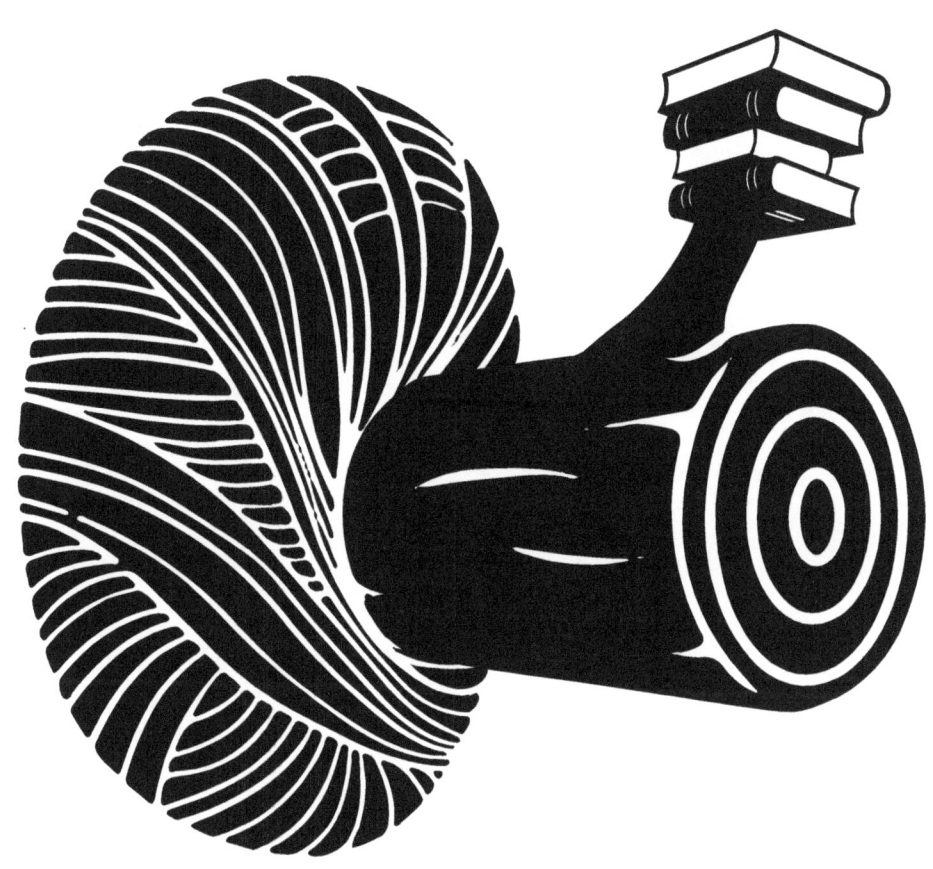

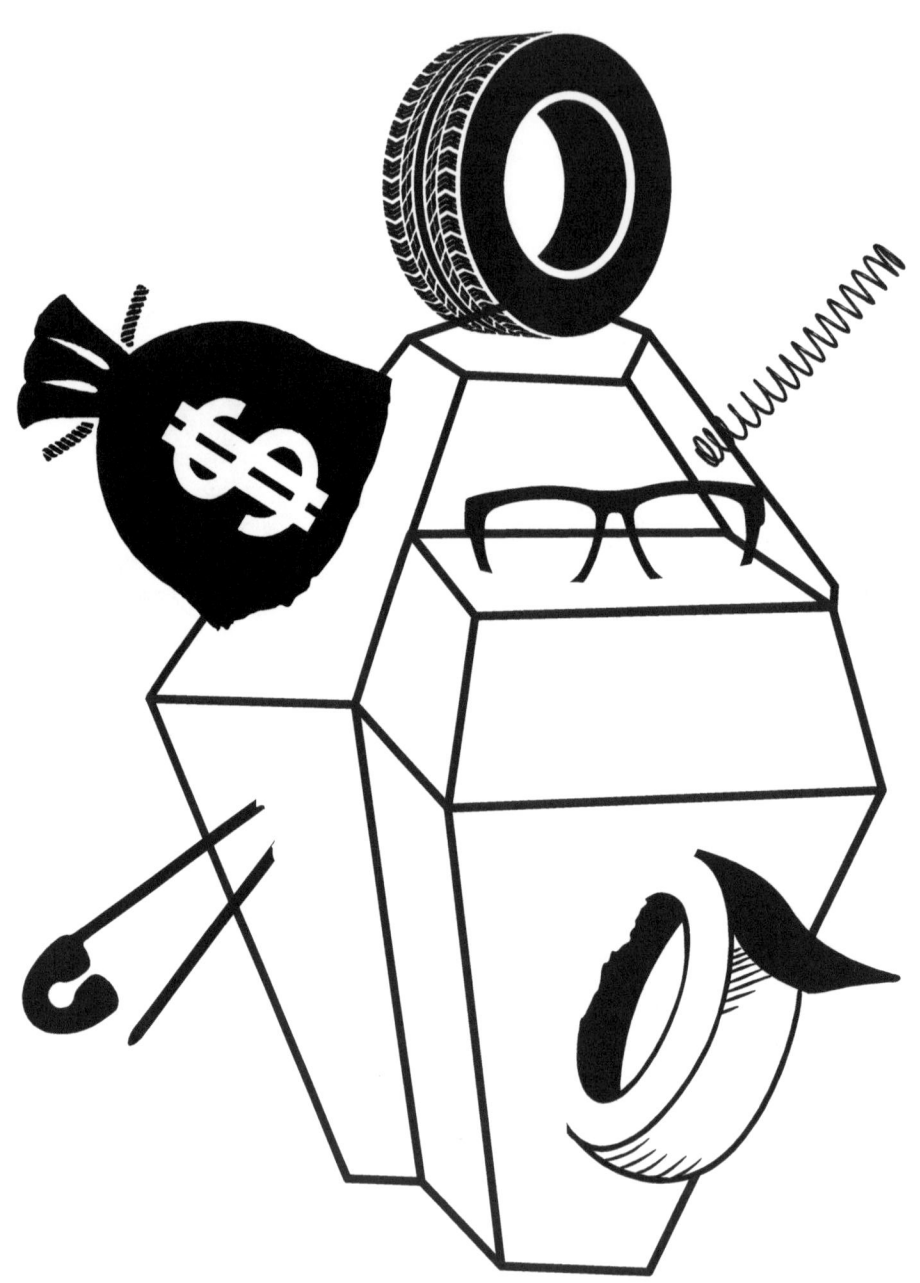

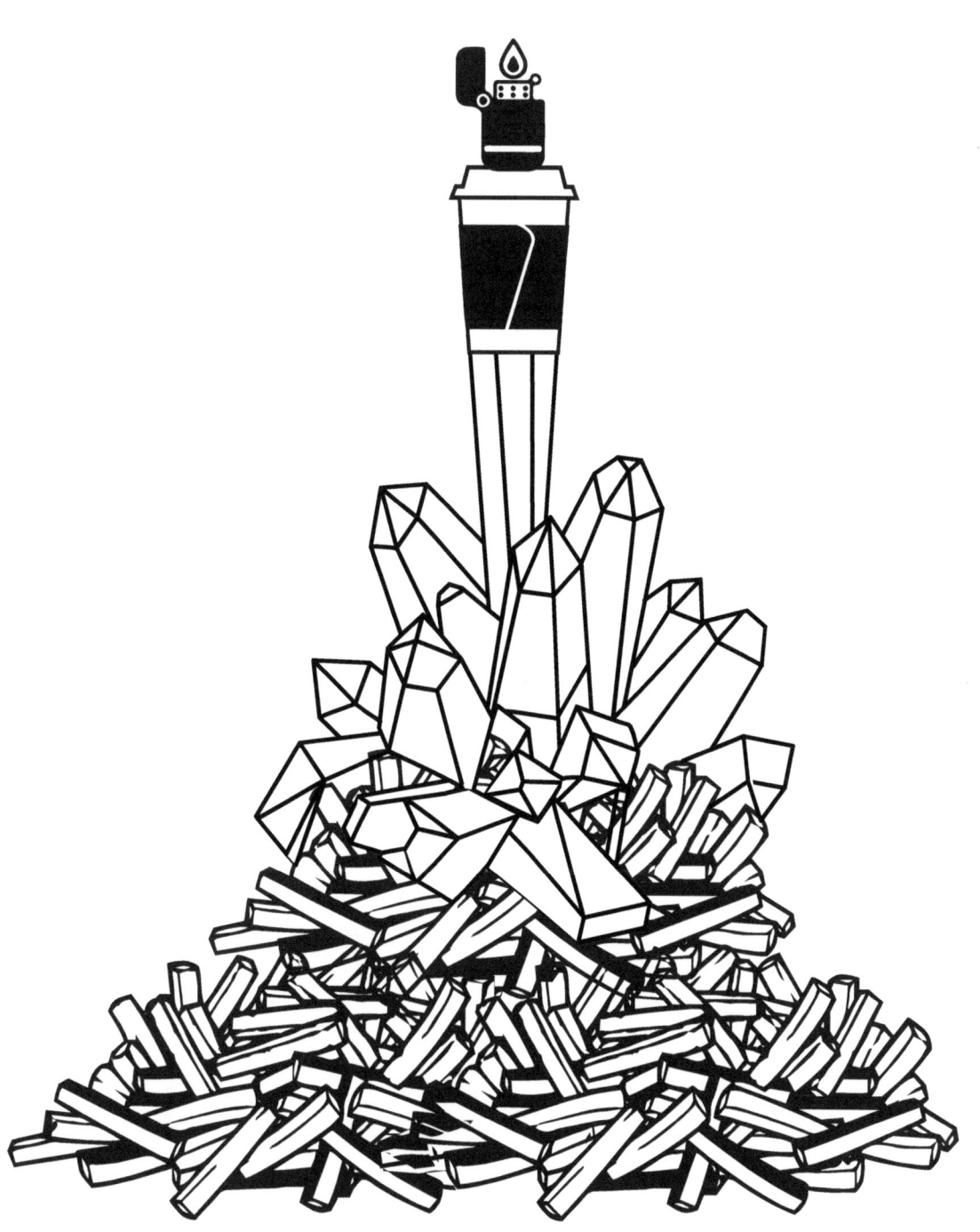

MARINA ZURKOW is a media artist focused on near-impossible nature and culture intersections. She uses life science, materials, and technologies to foster intimate connections between people and non-human agents.

Recent solo exhibitions of her work include bitforms gallery in New York; Chronus Art Center, Shanghai; the Montclair Art Museum, New Jersey; Diverseworks, Houston; her work has also been featured at FACT, Liverpool; San Francisco Museum of Modern Art; Walker Art Center, Minneapolis; Smithsonian American Art Museum, Washington D.C.; Museum of Fine Arts, Houston; National Museum for Women in the Arts, Washington D.C.; Borusan Collection, Istanbul; Museum of the Moving Image, New York; The Kitchen, New York; Ars Electronica, Linz, Austria; Transmediale, Berlin; Eyebeam, New York; Sundance Film Festival, Utah; Rotterdam Film Festival, The Netherlands; and the Seoul Media City Biennial, Korea, among others.

Her public art engagements have been supported by Creative Time, New York; LACE, Los Angeles; The New Museum's Ideas City, New York; Northern Lights, Minneapolis; The Artist's Institute, New York; 01SJ Biennial, San Jose, California; Rice University, Houston; University of Minnesota, Minneapolis; and Baruch College, New York.

Zurkow is the recipient of a 2011 John Simon Guggenheim Memorial Fellowship, and has been granted awards from the New York Foundation for the Arts, New York State Council for the Arts, the Rockefeller Foundation, and Creative Capital. She is on full time faculty at NYU's Interactive Technology Program (ITP) in Tisch School of the Arts, and lives in Brooklyn, NY. She is represented by bitforms gallery.

KATHLEEN FORDE is a curator based in NYC and Istanbul. Forde is the artistic director at large for Borusan Contemporary, a collection-based space for media arts exhibitions, commissions and public programming in Istanbul. Concurrently she is working as an independent curator with various institutions both nationally and abroad.

From 2005 to 2012 Forde was the Curator of Time-Based Visual Arts at the Experimental Media and Performing Arts Center (EMPAC) in Troy, NY.

Prior to EMPAC, Forde was the Curatorial Director for Live Arts and New Media at the Goethe Institut Internaciones in Berlin and Munich.

She has written and/or curated on a freelance basis for various organizations, including the Eyebeam Center for Art and Technology; The University of Michigan Museum of Art (UMMA); Independent Curators International; The Transmediale Festival, Berlin; Kunstverein Dusseldorf and Cologne; VideoZone, Tel Aviv; the Rotterdam Film Festival; and the Philadelphia Museum of Art. She sits on the board of Issue Project Room, NY, and on the Advisory Committees for the SETI Institute Artist in Residence Program and the Moving Image Art Fair, Istanbul.

In 2010 Forde was a fellow in the 2010 Center for Curatorial Leadership (CCL) fellowship class and held an Alexander von Humboldt research scholarship in Berlin from 2002–2003. She earned an MA in Post-1945 Art and Theory from Goldsmiths College, University of London, and a BA in Communications and Art History from the Loyola College of Maryland

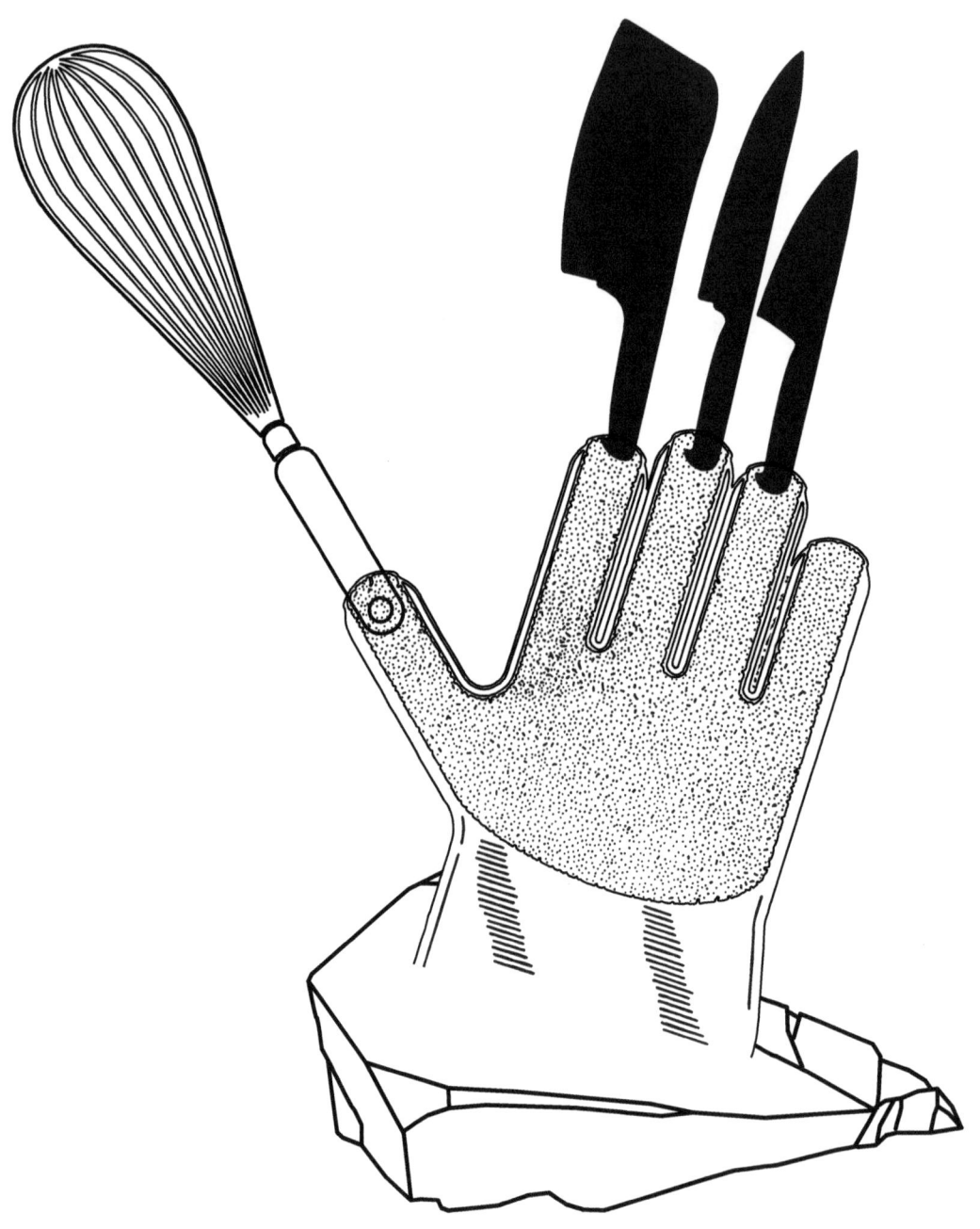